HOME REPAIR
AND IMPROVEMENT

WORKING WITH WOOD

BY THE EDITORS OF
TIME-LIFE BOOKS

TIME-LIFE BOOKS
ALEXANDRIA, VIRGINIA

Time-Life Books Inc.
is a wholly owned subsidiary of
TIME INCORPORATED

Founder   Henry R. Luce 1898-1967

Editor-in-Chief   Henry Anatole Grunwald
Chairman of the Board   Andrew Heiskell
President   James R. Shepley
Editorial Director   Ralph Graves
Vice Chairman   Arthur Temple

TIME-LIFE BOOKS INC.

Managing Editor   Jerry Korn
Executive Editor   David Maness
Assistant Managing Editors   Dale M. Brown (planning), George Constable, George G. Daniels (acting), Martin Mann, John Paul Porter
Art Director   Tom Suzuki
Chief of Research   David L. Harrison
Director of Photography   Robert G. Mason
Senior Text Editor   Diana Hirsh
Assistant Art Director   Arnold C. Hoieywell
Assistant Chief of Research   Carolyn L. Sackett
Assistant Director of Photography   Dolores A. Littles

Chairman   Joan D. Manley
President   John D. McSweeney
Executive Vice Presidents   Carl G. Jaeger, John Steven Maxwell, David J. Walsh
Vice Presidents   Nicholas Benton (public relations), John L. Canova (sales), Nicholas J. C. Ingleton (Asia), James L. Mercer (Europe/South Pacific), Herbert Sorkin (production), Paul R. Stewart (promotion), Peter G. Barnes
Personnel Director   Beatrice T. Dobie
Consumer Affairs Director   Carol Flaumenhaft
Comptroller   George Artandi

HOME REPAIR AND IMPROVEMENT

Editorial Staff for Working with Wood

Editor   William Frankel
Assistant Editor   David Thiemann
Designer   Kenneth E. Hancock
Picture Editor   Adrian Allen
Associate Designer   Daniel J. McSweeney
Text Editors   Russell B. Adams Jr., Leslie Marshall, Brooke Stoddard
Staff Writers   Lynn R. Addison, William C. Banks, Megan Barnett, Malachy Duffy, Steven J. Forbis, Bonnie Bohling Kreitler, William Worsley
Chief Researcher   Phyllis K. Wise
Art Associates   George Bell, Lorraine D. Rivard, Richard Whiting
Editorial Assistant   Susanne S. Trice

Editorial Production

Production Editor   Douglas B. Graham
Operations Manager   Gennaro C. Esposito, Gordon E. Buck (assistant)
Assistant Production Editor   Feliciano Madrid
Quality Control   Robert L. Young (director), James J. Cox (assistant), Michael G. Wight (associate)
Art Coordinator   Anne B. Landry
Copy Staff   Susan B. Galloway (chief), Margery duMond, Brian Miller, Celia Beattie
Picture Department   Renée DeSandies
Traffic   Jeanne Potter

Correspondents: Elisabeth Kraemer (Bonn); Margot Hapgood, Dorothy Bacon, Lesley Coleman (London); Susan Jonas, Lucy T. Voulgaris (New York); Maria Vincenza Aloisi, Josephine du Brusle (Paris); Ann Natanson (Rome). Valuable assistance was also given by Carolyn T. Chubet, Miriam Hsia (New York).

Ron Roszkiewicz, the chief consultant for this book, is an accomplished wood craftsman who develops tool specifications and prepares catalogs and instructional guides for a hand-tool supply company.

W. Flinn Settle is a carpenter specializing in custom-made home interiors.

Marc Shapiro, an amateur potter and glassblower, is a professional carpenter who specializes in the design and execution of home remodeling projects.

Danny J. Smith is an instructor of residential carpentry at the Arlington, Virginia, Career Center.

Roswell W. Ard is a consulting structural engineer and a professional home inspector in northern Michigan. He has written professional papers on wood-frame construction techniques.

Harris Mitchell, special consultant for Canada, has worked in the field of home repair and improvement for more than two decades. He is editor of the magazine *Canadian Homes* and author of a syndicated newspaper column, "You Wanted to Know," as well as a number of books on home improvement.

Library of Congress Cataloging in Publication Data
Time-Life Books.
   Working with wood.
   (Home repair and improvement; 18)
   Includes index.
   1. Carpentry—Amateurs' manuals. 2. House construction—Amateurs' manuals. 3. Dwellings—Maintenance and repair—Amateurs' manuals. I. Title.
TH5606.T55 694 79-13460
ISBN 0-8094-2428-2
ISBN 0-8094-2427-4 lib. bdg.

Contents

The Carpenter's Art

Wood is the ubiquitous building material. Nine of ten houses in the United States and Canada have wooden frames—and those that have walls of brick or stone often have a wooden skeleton. There is wood in floor joists and flooring, partitions, rafters and roof sheathing; and there is wood throughout the interior, in doors and doorframes, staircases, wall paneling, window sashes and molded trim.

Wood is the material of choice for good reasons: it is very strong, exceptionally durable, light in weight, weather-resistant and a good insulator. Furthermore, wood is beautiful, whether covered with paint or stained to emphasize its own striking patterns of color, texture, grain and shadow *(color portfolio, pages 32-40)*. And from the practical viewpoint of the carpenter, wood is universally avail-able, relatively inexpensive and capable of being shaped and assem-bled in an infinite variety of ways with simple tools.

The skills needed for working with wood are basic ones: sawing boards to size, making holes in them, shaping them with planes, spokeshaves, chisels and routers and joining the pieces neatly and securely with fasteners or glue. Nearly all eighth-grade boys—and these days, most girls—learn a smattering of these skills in a school shop class. But even those who have not forgotten what the shop teacher taught soon discover that he did not teach enough. The craftsmanship needed to repair or improve a house, from building foundation forms and rough framing to installing finish woodwork, is unlike that needed to build a napkin holder for the kitchen. House carpentry is more difficult: the work generally must be done free-hand, with portable tools and homemade jigs, rather than stationary power tools that guarantee precision; and construction lumber is rougher and less forgiving than the select boards that are used in a woodworking shop.

There are tricks to every basic operation—from the seemingly simple chores of driving a nail and planing a square, straight edge, to the complications of scribing an elaborate curve and joining fancy moldings—and mastery of those tricks distinguishes a good carpen-ter from an ordinary one. A generation ago, apprentice carpenters learned the nuances of their trade by watching and imitating a master—the sort of craftsman who walked onto the job a half hour early every morning, carrying a homemade wooden toolbox, to shoot the breeze and sharpen his tools. In this era of metal toolboxes and mass-produced houses, such perfectionists are a dying breed. But the keys to their craftsmanship—the small, critical techniques of han-dling tools the right way—remain the same. These techniques are not difficult to acquire. And once acquired, they make every carpentry job go fast and come out right.

The Carpenter's Material: Wood from Tree or Factory

"We may use wood with intelligence only if we understand it," architect Frank Lloyd Wright once said—and he spoke for craftsmen as well as architects. The quality of a carpenter's work depends as much on his knowledge of wood as on his skill with tools. Wood is a notoriously capricious material that can frustrate the finest workman—by tearing roughly when planed, perhaps, or by stubbornly refusing to accept a coat of paint.

Such problems are so common that many people accept them with resignation. In fact, trouble often can be prevented by choosing a wood (or a wood product, such as plywood) with its particular properties in mind.

You can learn a great deal about the strength and woodworking characteristics of a board simply by looking at it. At the end of a log or a board, you can see a series of thin, concentric circles. These annual rings, one formed each year during a spurt of growth, actually consist of a pair of rings: a light-colored one called earlywood or springwood, and a darker, denser one called latewood or summerwood. Boards with wide rings of earlywood generally are weaker than those in which latewood is predominant.

Trees are classified as softwoods or hardwoods. Hardwood lumber—which is used only for fine interior trim, flooring and paneling, because of its high cost—comes from broad-leaved trees, which drop their leaves every fall. Softwood lumber, from needle-leaved evergreen trees, is the builder's mainstay.

Lumbermen size softwood boards in several categories, such as board lumber, dimension lumber and timbers. When you order lumber, however, you need specify only the grade (a letter or number designation indicating the appearance and strength of a board), the species and the size—for example, a No. 2 spruce 2-by-10; the grade and the species generally are stamped on each board. As a general rule, order the lowest grade and cheapest species that are strong enough—and, in finish lumber, handsome enough—for the job (chart, pages 12-13). Higher grades than necessary represent a needless expense.

The sizes specified in ordering lumber are nominal rather than actual measurements. At one time, lumber sizes were based on the dimensions of green boards as they came from the sawmill, but lumber industry standards governing the sizes have changed with time. Today, a nominal 2-by-4 is actually 1½ inches by 3½ inches. The current nominal dimensions will match those of the lumber in a fairly modern house, but for an older house you may need to have boards cut to the correct width or buy slightly larger boards and cut them yourself (page 22).

When logs are sawed into boards at a mill, they contain a large amount of moisture. As this green lumber dries, its length remains virtually the same, but it tends to warp and to shrink in width and thickness: a green 2-by-10, for example, shrinks $\frac{1}{16}$ inch in thickness and $\frac{3}{8}$ inch in width. This is relatively unimportant in vertical wall studs, but in horizontal members—top and sole plates, joists and headers—it can cause sagging floors, cracked wallboard and popped nails. Always buy lumber that is stamped KD (for kiln-dried) or MC-15 (for a moisture content of only 15 per cent).

You may not be able to check each piece when you buy lumber, but when you select individual boards for a job, look for defects that impair its strength:
☐ Knots less than ¾ inch wide, common in virtually all rough lumber, do not weaken a board, although they may mar its appearance. Larger knots, particularly near the edge of a board, can weaken the board substantially. Such boards can be used for studs, firestops, blocking and similar jobs; they should not be used for load-bearing members such as posts, joists, rafters and headers.
☐ Cross-grained boards, in which the grain runs at an angle to the edge rather than parallel to it, are relatively weak; restrict them to nonbearing uses.
☐ Pith, the dark core of a tree trunk, weakens lumber; do not use boards with visible pith for structural lumber.
☐ Reaction wood—a section of a board with large gaps between annual rings and a rough, uneven grain—is found around many knots. It weakens the wood and is difficult to cut and shape with tools.
☐ Cracks in wood may be harmful or not, depending on their location. A shake—a wide crack between annual rings, caused by wind damage or decay—is a serious weakness. But checks, small cracks across the annual rings, are a purely cosmetic defect caused by uneven drying.

Factory-made wood products—particleboard, hardboard, fiberboard and plywood—are free of these defects and have several other advantages over ordinary boards, particularly for covering large surfaces. These products have consistent thickness and strength, and do not warp or shrink as much as wood.

Plywood, the most common of the four, is made by glueing together several thin sheets of wood called plies, with the grain of each ply at right angles to that of the adjacent ones. Two types are available: exterior, more expensive because it is made with a waterproof glue; and interior. The grade stamped on a plywood panel consists of two letters separated by a hyphen: the first letter identifies the face of the panel, the second identifies the back. Grade A is free of knots; grade B permits tight knots; grade C (the minimum allowed for exterior plywood) permits 1½-inch knotholes and some splits, and grade D permits knotholes up to 2½ inches wide.

Plywood intended for structural uses also is stamped with two numbers separated by a slash: the first number is the maximum rafter spacing for a sheet used as roof sheathing, the second is the maximum joist spacing for subflooring. Thus, a sheet labeled EXT C-C 32/16 would be exterior type, with up to 1½-inch knotholes on the face and back; it could be used on rafters spaced up to 32 inches apart or on joists up to 16 inches apart.

The other board products, weaker and less common than plywood, are made differently. Hardboard, sometimes used for siding, is manufactured by reducing wood to its individual fibers, then heating and compressing the fibers to form panels. It comes in two basic grades, Standard and Tempered; the latter has chemical additives to improve rigidity, hardness and strength. Fiberboard is made in the same way, but generally is impregnated with asphalt for weather-resistance. Particleboard—used for floor underlayment—is made by mixing wood particles with adhesives, then pressing the mixture into panels.

Watching for Warps

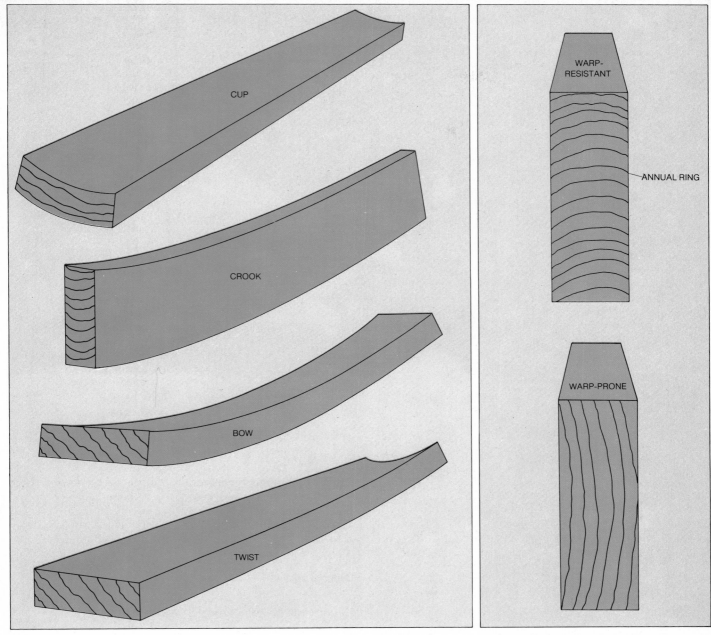

CUP

CROOK

BOW

TWIST

WARP-RESISTANT

ANNUAL RING

WARP-PRONE

Four types of warping. Check the straightness of a board by sighting along all four of its sides. A cup—a slight curve across the width of a board—does not seriously impair its strength or usefulness for construction. A board that has a crook (an end-to-end curve along an edge) or a bow (an end-to-end curve along a face) can be used horizontally with the convex side upward—the board will eventually straighten under the weight it bears—but should not be used vertically in a load-bearing wall. Boards with a twist are unstable and likely to distort more as they continue to dry; use them only if strength and straightness are unimportant, as in firestops.

Good and bad ends. Lumber with the annual rings—visible as thin, concentric lines at the end of a board—parallel to its edges resists warping. Boards with the rings parallel to the faces tend to warp from seasonal changes in humidity and temperature. Do not use them where appearance or straightness is critical—in the rough framing for a door or window, for example.

The Right Way
to Store Lumber

Stacking wood outdoors. Arrange lumber or plywood in tight stacks, raised 4 to 6 inches above the ground on scraps of 2-by-4, then cover the stacks with sheets of 4-mil plastic to keep moisture out. Use bricks on top of the sheeting and scrap lumber around its edges to anchor the cover loosely enough to let air circulate under the pile and remove condensation from the underside of the plastic. Use the wood within four months; otherwise the bottom boards may warp.

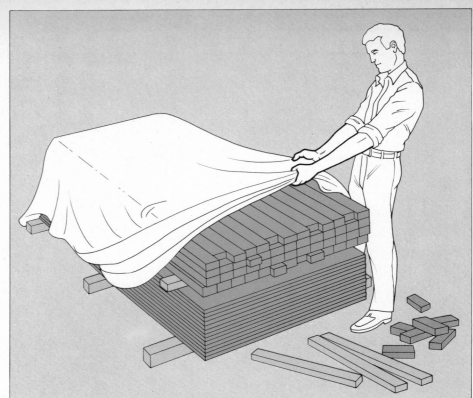

Racks for indoor storage. Build racks at 2-foot intervals; nail 2-by-4 uprights about 4 feet apart to a bottom plate, nail or bolt the bottom plate to the floor and nail the uprights to the exposed floor joists overhead or to a top plate fastened to the ceiling. Drill matching 1⅛-inch holes through each upright at 1-foot intervals and slide 1-inch steel pipes through the holes to support the lumber. Two racks will support boards up to 4 feet long; use three racks for lumber up to 8 feet and four racks for longer boards.

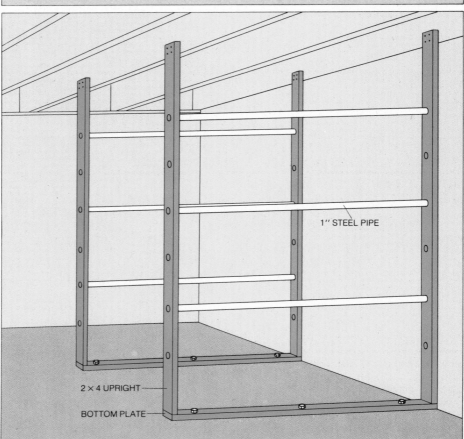

1″ STEEL PIPE

2 × 4 UPRIGHT

BOTTOM PLATE

The Qualities of Woods

Material	Characteristics
SOFTWOODS	
Cedar	Used for shingles and shakes, exterior siding and fence posts, because of its unusual resistance to rot and termites. Western varieties are light, soft and very weak; eastern are somewhat heavier and harder. Cedar is easy to shape with tools, is usually stable and bonds well with glue and paint; it does not hold nails well.
Fir, Douglas	The preferred softwood for load-bearing members such as girders and joists, because of its exceptional strength and relatively low cost. Douglas fir is a fairly heavy wood and holds fasteners well. It should not be used for visible woodwork or interior trim: it tends to split when exposed to the elements, does not take paint well and tears badly when shaped with tools.
Fir, true	A common material for rough framing. Fir is light in weight, fairly soft and slightly stronger than average. Although fir sometimes is used for interior trim and sashwork, it does not take paint or hold fasteners well.
Hemlock	Common for rough framing; often mixed with true fir and sold as HEM-FIR. Eastern varieties are light in weight, fairly hard and relatively weak; western ones are somewhat stronger. Hemlock tends to split and does not take paint or hold nails well.
Larch	A standard construction lumber, prized for its strength and nail-holding characteristics. It is heavy, fairly hard and quite rigid. This wood should not be used for exposed trim; it has many small knots, shrinks badly, splinters and tears when shaped with tools, and often splits when nailed. Larch boards are often mixed with Douglas fir and sold as LARCH-FIR.
Pine (except Southern pine)	The best softwoods for interior trim, because they are easy to shape and to finish; lower grades commonly used in rough framing. Pine is relatively light and about average in hardness and strength; it does not shrink or warp significantly as it dries, and it holds nails, glue and paint well.
Pine, Southern	Commonly used in stairways, girders and rough framing because of its great strength. Southern pine is heavy, harder than any other softwood, and very rigid; it shrinks a great deal as it dries but is stable afterward. This wood holds fasteners well, but is difficult to shape with tools, tends to split when exposed to the weather and does not hold paint well.
Redwood	Commonly used for girders, siding, fence posts, outdoor decks and shingles, because of its combination of beauty, strength and resistance to decay. Redwood is light, stable, fairly rigid and fairly hard; it is easy to shape with tools and to glue and paint. It ordinarily is used for exposed surfaces only, because of its high cost.
Spruce	Used primarily for rough framing. Spruce is light, soft and stable, with average strength. It is easy to shape with tools, bonds well with glue and holds fasteners well but is difficult to paint.
HARDWOODS	
Birch	Used for fine interior trim, doors and paneling. Birch is heavy, hard and strong; it is fairly easy to shape with tools, but tends to warp and, when nailed or screwed, to split. It does not bond well with paint or glue; clear finishes are generally used.
Oak	The most common hardwood for flooring, doors, paneling and interior trim, because of its hardness and reasonable cost. Oak is heavy, hard and very strong; it is difficult to shape with tools and does not bond well with glue. This wood holds nails well, although it tends to split when nailed; pilot holes must be used.
BOARD PRODUCTS	
Fiberboard	Used as insulation and sheathing for exterior walls. Fiberboard is light, soft, fairly flexible and very weak. It is easy to cut with tools and to glue, but does not hold nails and tends to shred when cut.
Hardboard	Used for siding, interior paneling and floor underlayment. Hardboard is fairly heavy, hard, and somewhat brittle. It is easy to shape with tools, though it shreds when cut; it takes glue and paint well but does not hold fasteners.
Particleboard	Used for underlayment and shelving; sometimes called chipboard or flakeboard. Particleboard is generally heavier and slightly stronger than hardboard. Panels can be cut and glued easily but tend to split when nailed on the edges and are difficult to paint.
Plywood	Used for subflooring, wall and roof sheathing, exterior siding, interior paneling and shelving. Heavy, fairly hard and much stronger than the other board products, plywood is easy to cut and shape with tools, and takes glue well; fasteners hold well when driven into the face, poorly when driven into the edge.

Special properties for special needs. The first column of this chart lists the woods and wood products commonly used in house construction, grouped in three categories: softwoods, hardwoods and board products (such as plywood). The second describes the applications and characteristics of each wood: weight, softness, strength, nail-holding characteristics and the like. Woods that do not respond to changes of humidity are called stable; if a wood tends to swell, warp or split when the humidity changes, the particular fault is indicated. Materials, grades and sizes of wood for specific jobs of house carpentry are given in the chart on pages 12-13. To use the chart, match the characteristics of the woods available in your area to the requirements of your job. For example, decay-resistant woods such as redwood and cypress are good choices for an outdoor deck; Douglas fir and Southern pine are best for important structural parts of a house because of their strength.

Matching the Material to the Job

Component	Material	Grade	Sizes	Comments
Bridging between joists:				
Diagonal	Softwood	Construction or No. 2 Common	1×3 or 1×4	Usually cut from scrap 1″ boards.
Solid	Softwood	No. 2	2×8, 2×10, 2×12	Cut from joist material.
Carriage, stair	Structural softwood	Select Structural	2×12	
Collar beam	Softwood	No. 2 Common or Construction	1×6, 2×4 or 2×6	Size depends on roof load and rafter span.
Deck, outdoor	Redwood, cedar or cypress	Appearance or Select Structural	2×4 or 2×6	
Fascia board	Softwood	Clear or No. 1 Common	1×6 or 1×8	
Firestop	Softwood	Construction or Standard	2×4 or 2×6	Usually cut from stud material.
Flooring	Hardwood	Clear or Select	¾″ thick, various widths.	No. 1 and No. 2 Common grades also available.
Furring strips	Softwood	No. 3 Common	1×2 or 1×3	
Girder, built-up	Structural softwood	No. 1 or No. 2	2×10 or 2×12	Straight lumber is essential; use boards side by side.
Header, plywood sandwich:				
Bearing	Structural softwood	No. 1	2×4 (doubled) 2×6 (doubled) 2×8 (doubled) 2×10 (doubled)	Spans to 4 feet Spans to 6 feet Spans to 8 feet Spans to 10 feet
Nonbearing	Structural softwood	No. 2	2×4 (doubled) 2×6 (doubled)	Spans to 5 feet Spans to 8 feet
Joist	Structural softwood	No. 1 or No. 2	2×8 2×10 2×12	Spans to 11 feet Spans to 14 feet Spans to 16 feet
Plate:				
Top or sole	Softwood	No. 2	2×4 or 2×6	Straight lumber is essential; use full-length pieces if possible.
Sill	Softwood	No. 2	2×4 or 2×6	Use long, straight pieces of pressure-treated lumber.
Post (for girder)	Structural softwood	No. 1	4×4 or 4×6	Soak the base of each post in commercial preservative.
Rafter	Structural softwood	No. 1 or No. 2	2×6 2×8 2×10	Spans to 9 feet Spans to 15 feet Spans to 20 feet
Ridge beam	Structural softwood	No. 2 Common	1″ lumber	Should be 2″ wider than rafters.

Component	Material	Grade	Sizes	Comments
Riser, stair	Oak or Southern pine	Clear	¾'' thick	Use No. 2 grade for risers concealed by carpeting.
Sheathing:				
Roof	Exterior plywood	C-D	⅜'', ½'' or ⅝'' thick	Thickness depends on roof load; permissible joist spacing stamped on sheet.
Wall	Interior plywood	C-D	$5/16$'', ⅜'' or ½'' thick	Thickness depends on stud spacing and wall material; use type CDX where weather is severe.
	Asphalt-impregnated fiberboard	Regular density	½''	Used primarily on new construction.
Shelving (rough)	Pine	Clear or No. 2 Common	1 × 8, 1 × 10 or 1 × 12	Shelf supports must be less than 32'' apart.
	Interior plywood	A-C or A-D	½'', ⅝'' or ¾''	Thickness depends on spacing of shelf supports.
	Particleboard	1-B-1	½'', ⅝'' or ¾''	Thickness depends on spacing of shelf supports.
Studs	Softwood	Stud or utility stud	2 × 4	Available only in lengths less than 10 feet; use Construction grade for longer pieces.
		No. 2	2 × 6	
Subflooring	Interior plywood	B-D or C-D plugged	¾''	Use exterior plywood in bathrooms, kitchens and laundries where subfloor will be exposed to weather during construction.
Tread, stair	Oak or Southern pine	Clear	1⅛'' thick	Use No. 2 grade for tread concealed by carpeting.
Underlayment	Particleboard	1-B-1	⅜'' to ¾''	
	Hardboard	Underlayment grade	¼'', $5/16$'' or ⅜''	
	Exterior plywood	C-C plugged	⅜'' to ¾''	Use in bathrooms, kitchens and laundries.

Matching the material to the job. The first column of this chart lists the components of the frame and flooring of a house. The second specifies the right material or gives a choice of materials to use for each component when building or renovating. In this column the generic term ''softwood'' stands for a variety of suitable woods, including larch, fir, Douglas fir, hemlock and pine; use the one that is least expensive in your locality. The term ''structural softwood,'' specified for such load-bearing components as joists and rafters, indicates that the strength of a board is critical; use the strongest softwood available, generally Douglas fir or Southern pine. For ''hardwood,'' oak is the most common choice, but other woods can also be used (chart, page 11).

The third column gives the minimum grade suitable for each component, in the terms most commonly used to order boards from a lumberyard; if the salesmen in your area use different terms, ask for the equivalent of the grades given here. The fourth column recommends sizes of boards for each component. Wherever these dimensions are matched to a span, as in joists, headers and rafters, the chart can be used only as a general guide; consult an architect, a structural engineer or your local building code to check the exact size you need.

A Clean and Simple Cut across the Grain

A cut straight across the grain of wood is the most common cut in carpentry, for a simple reason: the grain runs with the length of a board and standard-length boards generally must be shortened. Fortunately, such crosscutting, at 90° to the board edge, is also the easiest cut: it is generally a short one, and the teeth of a crosscut-saw blade need only slice the wood fibers, a cut that requires less effort than the scraping and ripping performed by a rip saw *(pages 22-27)*.

Which tool to use for crosscutting depends on the precision required and the volume and location of the job.

Most of these cuts—particularly in framing lumber—can be made with a portable electric circular saw. For precise work on trim, you need a stiff-bladed backsaw and a miter box. Both rough and precise cuts across the grain can be made quickly and easily with a radial-arm power saw *(pages 19-21)*. The crosscut handsaw is still sometimes necessary—for rough cuts in cramped areas, for jobs where there is no electricity, and for boards that are too short to be steadied safely for a power saw.

When you buy new tools, there are certain features to look for. The teeth of a crosscut handsaw are set alternately to the left and right of the plane of the blade, and are not only pointed, but also beveled front to back *(page 56)*. A better blade is also wider near the teeth, to keep the kerf from binding the blade. A blade with 10 teeth—"points"—per inch is generally useful; an 8-point saw makes quicker but rougher cuts.

While every carpenter owns a handsaw, he most often uses a portable circular saw, which makes rough cuts nearly instantly and, with a simple jig, cuts lengths very accurately. A model with a 1½-horsepower motor and a blade of 7¼-inch diameter, which can saw completely through a 2-by-4 at a 45° angle, is adequate for home use. Some models have special safety features, such as a brake that stops the blade quickly when the trigger switch is released. All, however, are very dangerous tools, and must be used with careful attention to safety.

The multipurpose blade that comes with most circular saws, its teeth a compromise between the designs used for crosscut and rip handsaws, is excellent for crosscutting. If you do a great deal of cutting, however, you may want to substitute a more expensive blade that has carbide tips brazed to its teeth—the carbide-tipped blade makes a slightly wider kerf than an ordinary steel one, but it stays sharp more than 10 times as long. For especially smooth cuts, use a hollow-ground steel blade *(page 59)*. Set the cutting depth for any of these blades so that one entire tooth will protrude below the bottom of the board you cut.

Even in a jig, a circular saw cannot match the accuracy of a miter box guiding a backsaw, its fine-toothed blade reinforced to keep the cut straight. For good work you need more than the simple, slotted box of wood or plastic that sells for a few dollars. Versatile models like the one on the cover—made of metal and able to accommodate boards 3 to 4 inches thick and 4 to 8 inches wide at any angle—are available at prices that range from modest to high. In them, the saw slides within guides and can be locked in a raised position while you align a board on the frame below. Any miter box should be anchored to a workbench; use bolts and wing nuts so that it can be easily removed for work elsewhere.

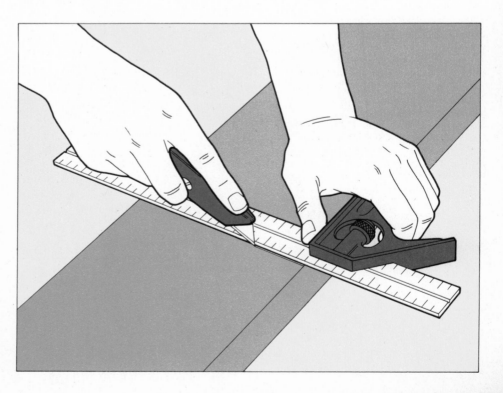

Marking a crosscut. For most 90° crosscuts, hold the handle of a combination square firmly against the edge of the board and mark along the blade. For rough work, use a pencil; for finer work, score the wood several times with the point of a utility knife—the scored line is sharper and helps prevent splintering as the wood is cut.

Crosscutting with a Handsaw

1 Beginning the cut. Lay a board across two sawhorses, steady it with the knee opposite your cutting arm and grip the handle of the saw so that your index finger rests along the blade to help keep the saw course true. Set the heel, or handle end, of the blade on the board edge at an angle of about 20°. For rough work, the teeth should lie directly on a penciled line; for fine work, on the waste side of a knife mark.

Holding the thumb of your free hand against the blade as a guide, draw the saw halfway back toward you, pressing lightly to cut into the wood. Lift the blade from the wood, reset it to the starting position, and then pull backward again; do this several times until the kerf is at least as deep as the teeth. Then lengthen and deepen the kerf with short, smooth back-and-forth strokes that cut in both directions.

2 Cutting through the board. When the kerf is about an inch long—sufficient to establish the direction of the cut—pull your index finger back to help grip the handle, gradually increase the angle of the saw to 45° and lengthen your strokes, cutting mainly on the forward stroke and using moderate pressure. Use most of the full length of the saw, from about 3 inches from the tip nearly to the handle. When the cut is almost complete, reach over the top of the saw to support the waste piece so that it does not fall and splinter the wood.

If the saw binds in green or warped wood, rub paraffin on the blade or drive a wedge into the kerf behind the blade. If the blade twists and binds as you attempt to correct a straying cut, either begin the cut at a new spot or widen the old kerf by resawing it until you reach uncut wood.

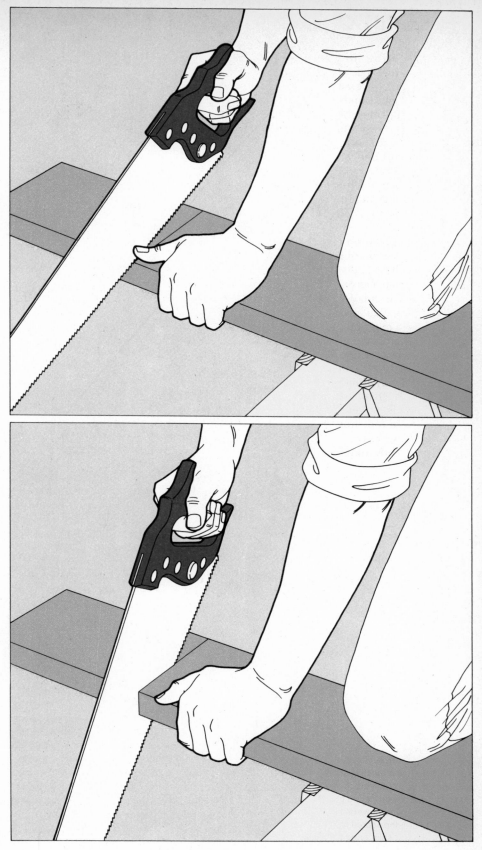

Safety Tips for Circular-Saw Crosscutting

Using a circular saw demands the utmost care. Follow the standard power-tool safety rules: wear goggles; do not wear loose clothing, a necktie or jewelry; keep children, pets and clutter out of your work area; use a grounded outlet for tools with three-wire cords. But also take extra precautions:

□ Never place your fingers beneath a board being cut.

□ Unplug the saw when adjusting or changing blades.

□ Do not stand right behind the saw; if the blade binds, the saw may leap back.

□ Never carry the saw with your finger on the trigger.

□ Before setting the saw down, check to see that the blade guard is closed.

Freehand Cuts with a Circular Saw

1 Aligning the saw. Lay the board across two sawhorses and steady it with either a foot or a knee, depending on the height of the sawhorses and your sense of balance. Place the front of the base plate on the board with the blade at least ½ inch from the board edge, and hold the saw so that entire plate is level; then use the guide in the base plate, or the blade itself, to align the blade with the cutting line.

The guide in the base plate is generally an effective device for aligning a straight cut, but after you change or sharpen the blade, the guide itself may not line up properly with the teeth of the blade. Experience with your own saw will tell you how to compensate for a misaligned base-plate guide or whether to use it at all.

2 Making the cut. Start the saw and, applying pressure forward but not downward, push the blade smoothly into the board, watching the guide or blade to be sure that the blade cuts along the line. Near the end of the cut, slow the forward motion, then quickly push through the remainder of the board in a single stroke. Immediately release the switch and move the saw away from the board, checking to be certain that the blade guard returns to its closed position.

If the blade binds or goes off course, release the switch immediately. Pull the blade from the kerf, reset it to the starting position and start sawing again, cutting slowly into the kerf. Allow the blade to work its own way—with minimal pressure forward—through the wood that was binding it before, or through new wood along the cutting line to correct a wayward first cut.

A Guide and a Jig
for Accurate Speed

A square for right angles. Hold the long leg of a carpenter's square against the far edge of the board and set the base plate against the outer edge of the short leg. Slide saw and square along the board until the blade aligns with the cutting line, then make the cut by moving the saw along the short leg of the square.

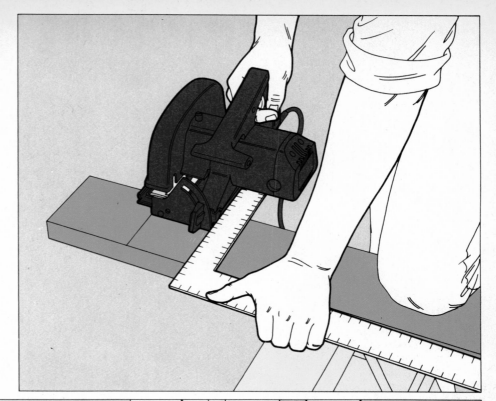

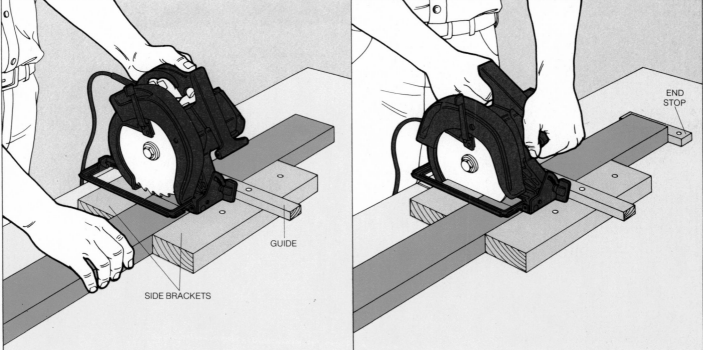

A jig for cuts of equal length. Set the marked board that you are going to cut on a sheet of plywood, and bracket it with two long wood scraps as thick as the piece to be cut; nail these side brackets to the plywood. Nail a wood-strip guide across the top of the scraps at right angles to the board and set the saw, with its blade fully elevated, against the guide (*left*). Slide the board beneath the saw until the cutting line is below the blade; then, at the far end of the board, nail a block of wood to the plywood as an end stop. Set the blade to the proper depth and cut through the board and the side brackets by running the saw along the guide (*right*). To cut more boards to the same length, slip one at a time into the jig and against the stop.

To cut several pieces at once—for example, to cut boards for fence pickets—widen the jig to hold the pieces side by side and make a long stop exactly parallel to the guide.

A Miter Box for Precision

1 **Setting the angle.** With the blade raised, release the catch of the miter box's angle-setting knob and move the pointer to the 90° mark. Position the cutting line of the board approximately beneath the blade, release the front and back saw-guide catches and then, holding the blade ¼ inch above the board, make a final adjustment in the position of the cutting line.

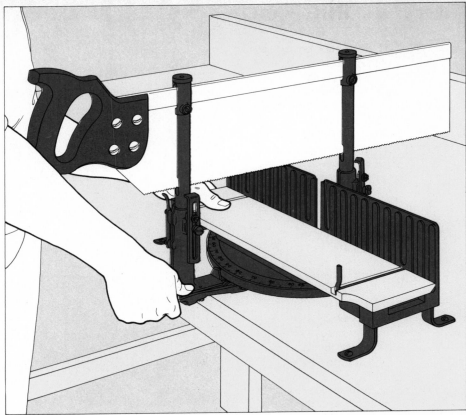

2 **Making the cut.** With the thumb of your free hand, steady the board against the frame. Begin the kerf with several backward strokes, as for any crosscut, but hold the saw level to cut the entire upper surface of the wood along the cutting line. Then, cutting on both forward and backward strokes, cut the rest of the way through the board. Use long, smooth strokes that fall just short of pulling the blade from the rear guide or running the handle into the front guide.

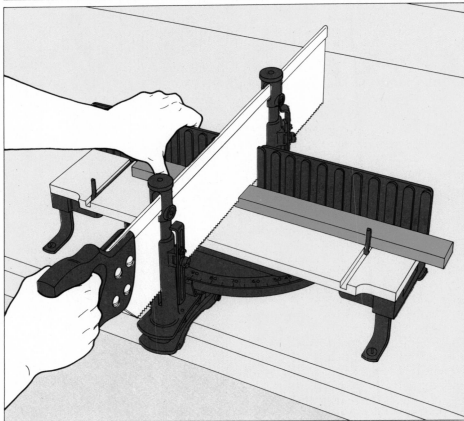

The Versatile Radial Arm Saw

The multijointed stationary power tool called a radial arm saw is one of the most versatile, useful and ingeniously designed of all machines for working with wood. While it is expensive—5 to 10 times the price of a portable circular saw—it can make any cut that could be made with a handsaw, circular saw or miter box, but with a combination of speed and precision that is not found in any one of the other tools. It is the preferred shop tool for carpentry; it is better adapted than a table saw for cutting many boards to the same length and angle, as in rough framing, or for making many cuts through large pieces of trim.

The blade and motor of the saw ride above a worktable along the track of a horizontal arm. Cutting is always above the table, where the blade position is clearly visible, and crosscutting is simple—you pull the saw by its handle straight toward you until the board is cut, then push the saw back. But the arm that supports the saw can also pivot more than 180° over the table and the saw can tilt on this arm to any angle: the pivoting and tilting together can position the blade for a cut at any angle. Scales and locks are used to adjust the blade settings with the accuracy of a miter box; safety guards shield the blade itself.

Crosscutting blades for a radial arm saw include the standard multipurpose steel blade and the long-lasting carbide-tipped blade, both described on page 14. For fine cutting, especially for trim, use a planer blade, which is slower but makes an extremely smooth cut.

Most radial arm saws come equipped with a warp-resistant particleboard table top. Protect this table surface—which otherwise will be gouged as the blade penetrates the first board being cut—with a layer of ¼-inch plywood secured with rubber cement. Cover the edges of the plywood with masking tape, to prevent splinters from snagging your clothes. Set tables at the sides of the saw to support long boards.

Since both the plywood cover on the table surface and the replaceable wooden "fence" that helps to hold boards in place are going to be cut by the blade in use, many craftsmen prepare the cover and the fence for use by making cross-cuts, angle cuts *(page 28)* and rip cuts *(page 24)* in them in advance. Such preparatory cuts will then help the user to align boards for accurate cutting.

In addition to the plywood cover, there are other accessories that increase the saw's usefulness. A wooden block placed as a stop at a fixed distance from the blade helps when you need to cut many pieces to the same length. An extra-tall guide, or fence, used as a temporary replacement for the standard fence helps when you need to cut accurately through several boards simultaneously.

Anatomy of a Radial Arm Saw

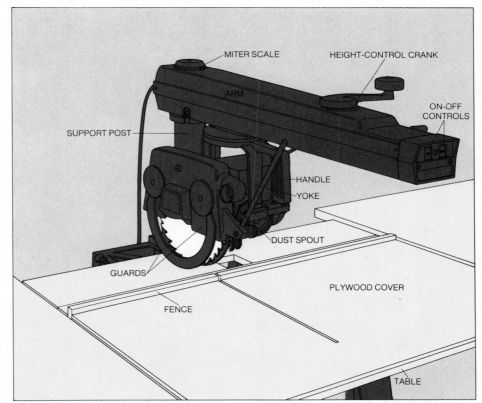

A versatile cutter. This saw, whose teeth cut downward and away from you, is suspended with its motor in a yoke that permits it to tilt 100° right or left. The yoke also can turn more than 360° in its swivel mount, which rides in a track beneath a horizontal arm. The arm can move as well—manually 105° to both right and left, or up and down when you turn a height-control crank that adjusts the arm's support post. A miter scale shows the angle of the blade in relation to a replaceable wooden fence against which the board to be cut is set. A replaceable plywood sheet covers the worktable.

In use the saw is pulled from back to front along its track in the arm, the blade cutting through first the fence and then the board as it skims the plywood table cover. Upper and lower guards shield the blade, and a dust spout directs sawdust to the side. Other scales, locks and safety features are provided for angle cuts *(pages 28-31)* and rip cuts *(pages 22-27)*.

The Basic Setup
for a Crosscut

1 **Setting up the job.** With the motor off and in
the rear position, set the arm at 0° on the miter
scale and the blade ⅛ inch below the level of
the plywood table covering. Place the board
against the fence, positioned so that the blade
will cut on the waste side of the cutting line. Rest
the fingers of your left hand on the board at
least 6 inches from the cutting line, and press the
board against the fence with your thumb.

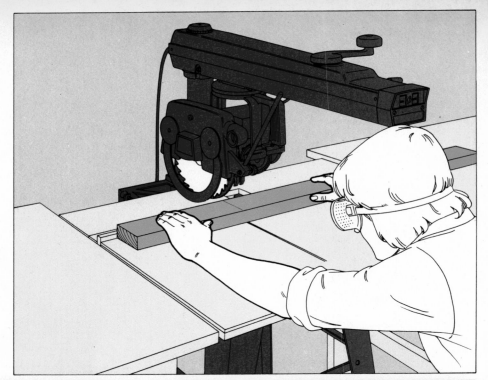

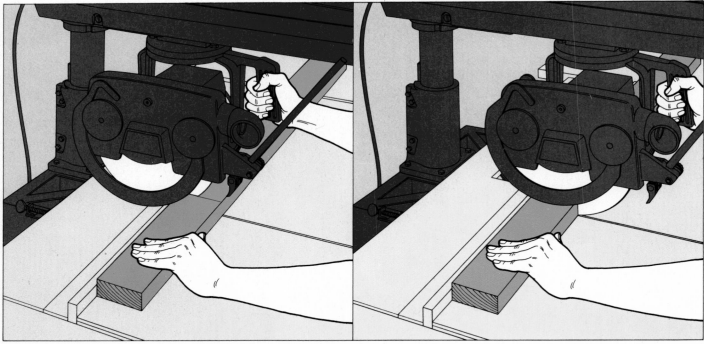

2 **Making the cut.** Start the motor and, keeping
a firm grip on the handle, pull the saw into the
board (left); if the blade tends to climb over
the board and bind there, lock your elbow by
straightening your arm. When the bottom of
the blade emerges from the front edge of the
board (right), return the saw to the rear position and shut off the power. If you pull the blade
completely through the cut board, the saw
teeth moving upward at the rear may catch the
waste piece and hurl it over the fence.

If you cannot keep the blade from climbing over
the board, shut off the power at once, then
start the cut again, this time in two passes. For
the first pass, raise the blade to make a kerf
about half as deep as the board; for the second,
position the saw at the normal cutting height.

Special Setups
for Awkward Jobs

Stops for repeated cuts. To crosscut a number of long boards one after the other to the same length, nail a 2-by-4 block that is chamfered—beveled—at the bottom to keep sawdust from building up and distorting your measurement, to a worktable at the side of the saw (*left*). The block will serve as a stop, as in cuts made with a circular saw (*page 17, bottom*).

As a stop for short boards, fasten a woodworker's clamp to the saw fence, leaving a gap below the clamp for accumulations of sawdust (*right*).

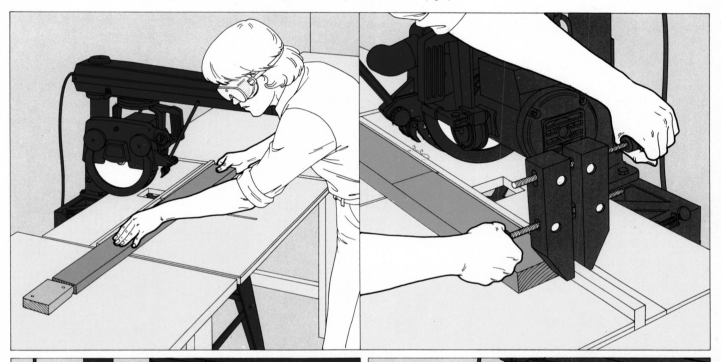

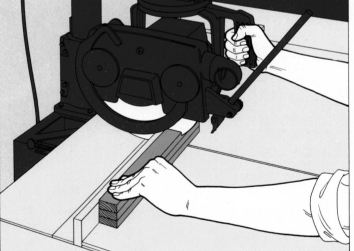

A tall fence for multiple cutting. To cut a number of boards in one pass, stack them against a taller replacement for the standard fence—use a 1-by-3 or a strip of plywood or particleboard ¾ inch thick and 3 inches wide.

Cutting thick lumber. To crosscut a board that is as much as twice as thick as the distance between motor and blade teeth, raise the blade until the motor clears the board to be cut, then make a first cut. Turn the board over, align the kerf you have made in it with the blade, and pull the saw through for the final cut.

Sawing with the Grain for a Rip Cut

Cutting a board lengthwise, with the grain, in what is known as rip cutting, used to be a major part of a carpenter's work. It is so no longer—modern sawmills cut and plane boards to the standard dimensions of house carpentry—but many boards still must be trimmed to width on the job. Among them are furring strips, stair treads and risers, odd-sized jambs for plaster walls, and new studs cut to match old, full-sized lumber.

None of these jobs are easy. A rip cut, which scrapes and tears the fibers of a board, requires about five times as much work as a crosscut, which neatly severs the fibers. It is harder to keep straight, because the saw blade tends to follow the grain, which is never quite true. And it leaves a rough edge that must be planed smooth on exposed pieces of wood; in marking such pieces for a cut, allow an extra $1/16$ inch for the planing.

Most rip cuts are now made with power saws, but a handsaw remains the only suitable tool when a board already is nailed in place in a hard-to-reach spot, or when a piece of wood is too small to be cut safely with a power saw. The preferred hand tool is a 5½- or 6-point ripsaw, which has teeth designed specifically for efficient rip cuts (opposite, top); an alternative is an 8-point crosscut saw, slower but more commonly available.

A portable circular saw, the standard ripping tool, is fast and durable but not particularly precise, even in skilled hands, when the cut is made freehand. For somewhat more accurate results, you can use the rip guide shown overleaf; on boards more than 12 inches wide, use one of the panel-cutting guides shown on pages 42-43. For all of these cutting methods, the power saw is fitted with the same blades that are used for crosscutting—a steel combination blade (or its carbide-tipped equivalent) for rough cuts and a hollow-ground planer blade for somewhat smoother ones. Pitch and resins gradually build up on either type of blade until it sticks in the kerf; these deposits are easy to remove with kerosene or commercial solvents.

The radial arm saw, best for both production and precision, can rip with these blades, but for easier, cleaner cuts with this shop tool you may prefer to buy a special rip blade, which has chisel-shaped teeth with deep recesses between them. The saw is easily set up for ripping (pages 24-27), but to cut long pieces, you will need to slide boards along worktables that you have placed on each side of the saw table.

Three Ways to Mark for a Rip

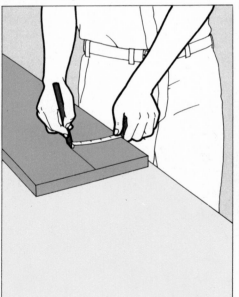

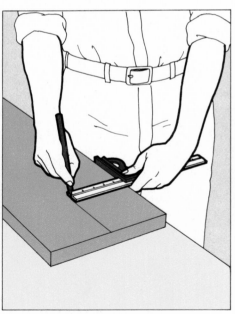

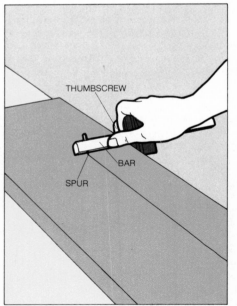

A steel tape for rough work. Hold the tape case in the palm of one hand, extend the tape to the measurement for the cut, and set the case next to the edge of the board, with your forefinger tight against the edge; with the fingers of your other hand, hold a pencil against the end of the tape—many tapes have a V-shaped notch there. Slide both hands smoothly along the boards; use your forefinger as a guide, keep the tape perpendicular to the edge and keep the length constant by clamping your fingers firmly on the tape.

A combination square for convenience. Extend the blade of the square to the measurement for the cut and lock it with the knurled nut in the handle. Set the square, machined face of the handle tight against the edge of the board with one hand and hold a pencil against the end of the blade with the other; many blades have a groove here that will help hold the pencil. Slide the square and pencil along the board together to mark the cut, holding the machined face of the square tight against the edge of the board.

A marking gauge for precision. Mark the start of the cut at one end of the board. Hold the head of the marking gauge flat against the edge of the board, slide the bar out until its spur touches the mark and tighten the thumbscrew on the head. Hold the head of the gauge in your palm and roll it forward until the spur barely touches the board, then push the gauge along the board; press the head firmly sideways against the edge and brace the bar with your thumb. The spur should score a clear, shallow line.

The Old-fashioned Way: Ripping with a Handsaw

Using a ripsaw. Set a small board on a saw-horse as you would for a crosscut; support a large one between two sawhorses. Start the cut as you would a crosscut *(page 15, Step 1)*; then, when the cut is about an inch long, raise the angle of the saw to about 60° and apply most of the force on the push stroke. If the blade buckles or skips through the cut, lower the angle of the saw slightly; if the board pinches the blade, tap wooden wedges into the kerf *(inset)*.

When using one sawhorse, edge the board forward little by little; halfway through the cut, turn the board around and saw from the other end. When using two sawhorses, cut to within a few inches of a horse, then slide the board back and resume cutting on the other side of the horse.

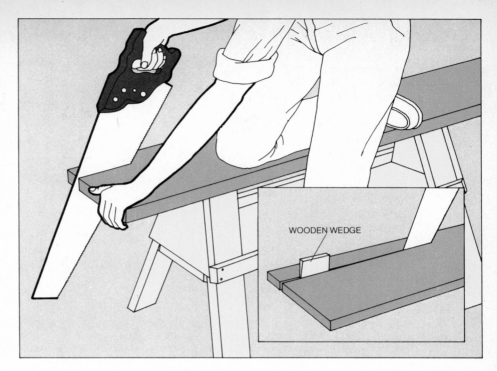

WOODEN WEDGE

Ripping with a Circular Saw

A freehand cut. Clamp or tack the board to two sawhorses and set the saw blade ¼ inch deeper than the thickness of the board. Rest the saw nose flat on the end of the board and align the base-plate guide mark or the blade itself with the cutting line, then start the saw and slowly push it into the board. Near the end of the cut, a base-plate guide mark will slide off the end of the board; guide the saw by the blade alone.

If the saw motor slows and labors, pause until it gains speed, then push it forward more slowly. If the cut goes off the line, angle the saw slightly toward the line for a few inches, then straighten it when the cut returns to the line. If the blade binds, turn off the saw and tap a wooden wedge into the kerf near the blade *(above, inset)*.

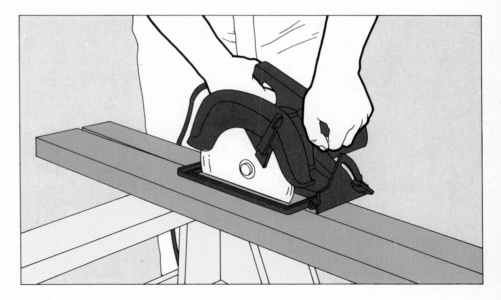

Safety Tips for Circular-Saw Rips

☐ Stand to one side of the saw, not directly behind it. If the saw kicks back—a common occurrence in a rip cut—your leg could be gashed.
☐ Do not rest your fingers on the kerf; it is the path of a possible kickback.

☐ Do not hold the waste piece with your hand; let the sawhorses support it or let it fall.
☐ Wear goggles to protect your eyes from the large amounts of sawdust filling the air around a rip cut.

Using a rip guide. With the saw unplugged, set the nose of the base plate flat on the board and align the blade with the marked line. Slide the arm of the guide through its base-plate holder until the guide shoe fits against the edge of the board, then tighten the guide arm in position. When you make the cut, maintain a gentle sideways pressure on the saw to keep the guide shoe tight against the edge of the board.

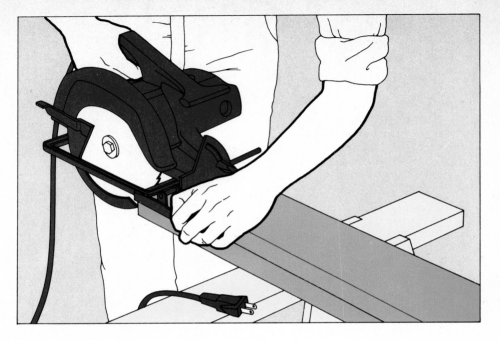

Ripping with a Radial Arm Saw

1 Setting the "in-rip" position. With the motor off and the blade depth set ⅛ inch below the table top, pull the saw forward to the end of the arm and tighten the rip lock. Start the motor, grip the saw handle with your left hand and release the yoke lock with your right. Pivot the motor slowly to the right with both hands, cutting a shallow quarter circle into the plywood table covering; at the end of the quarter circle, a cog in the yoke mechanism will lock the blade parallel to the fence, in the in-rip position, that is, with the motor away from the fence. Leave the motor on and proceed immediately to Step 2.

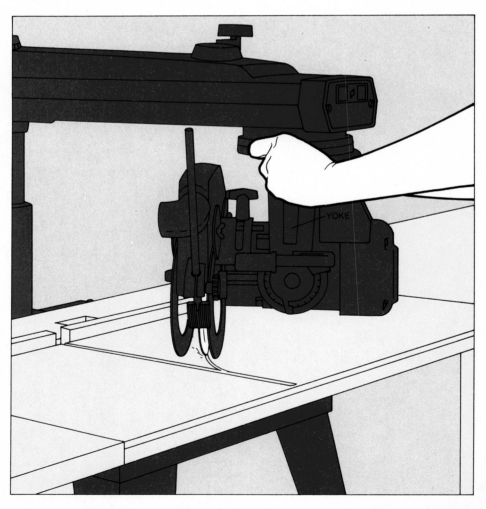

2 **Making the rip troughs.** Release the rip lock and, using both hands, slowly push the saw toward the back of the table, cutting a shallow trough in the table covering. When the blade guard reaches the fence, pull the yoke back to the end of the arm and tighten the rip lock.

Release the yoke lock and pivot the yoke 180° to the "out-rip" position (*inset*)—that is, put the motor next to the fence. Loosen the rip lock and slowly push the saw back, making a second trough that runs into the end of the first.

OUT-RIP POSITION

IN-RIP POSITION

RIP TROUGH

Setting the Saw and Making the Cut

1 **Setting the width of the cut.** Turn the saw motor off. To cut a width less than 8 inches, move the yoke to the in-rip position and lock the yoke clamp (*page 19, bottom*); for wider cuts, move the yoke to the out-rip position. Push the yoke along the arm until the pointer on the arm's rip scale shows the correct width and tighten the rip clamp. For absolute precision, lift the guard closest to the fence and measure the cut width between the fence and the edge of a blade tooth set toward the fence (*inset*).

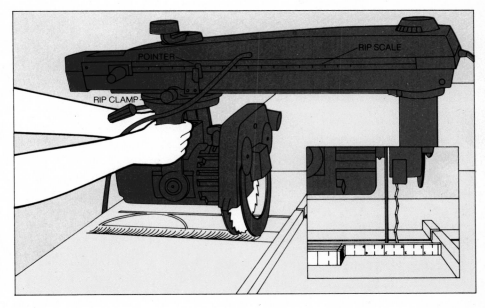

POINTER

RIP SCALE

RIP CLAMP

Safety Tips for Radial-Arm-Saw Rips

In addition to the basic safety rules on page 19, observe these precautions:
☐ Wear goggles.
☐ Set and test the guard and antikick-back fingers (*overleaf, Steps 2 and 3*) before you make a cut.
☐ Feed the saw from the right when in-ripping, the left when out-ripping.
☐ Stand beside, not behind, the board.
☐ Do not let a helper push the board against the fence on the far side of the blade; the pressure can pinch the kerf around the blade and cause a kickback.
☐ Keep your fingers at least 2 inches from the blade; never insert them underneath the guard.
☐ Do not reach near the blade to move the waste piece when the cut is completed; push it with a scrap of lumber or pull it from the other side of the blade.

2 **Adjusting the guard.** Place the board (or a scrap of the same thickness) beside the blade and loosen the wing nut that locks the guard to the motor. Rotate the guard until the spring clip on its nose is ⅛ inch above the board, then tighten the wing nut, locking the guard.

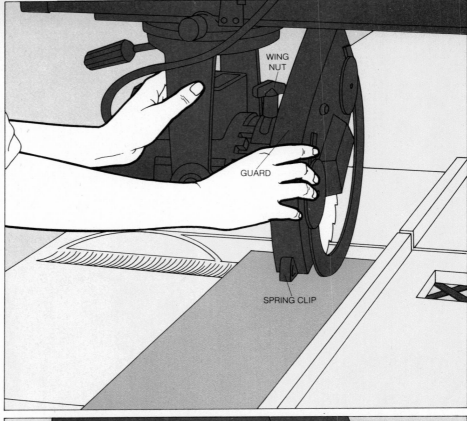

3 **Setting the antikickback fingers.** Place the board alongside the antikickback fingers at the back of the guard. The fingers hang from the end of a rod; loosen the clamp that fastens this rod to the guard, lower the rod until the fingers dangle ⅛ inch below the top of the board and tighten the clamp. To test the fingers, slide a board under them from the blade side, then try to push it back toward the blade (inset); the fingers should bite into the top of the board and prevent it from moving backward. If they do not grab the board, adjust the rod until they do.

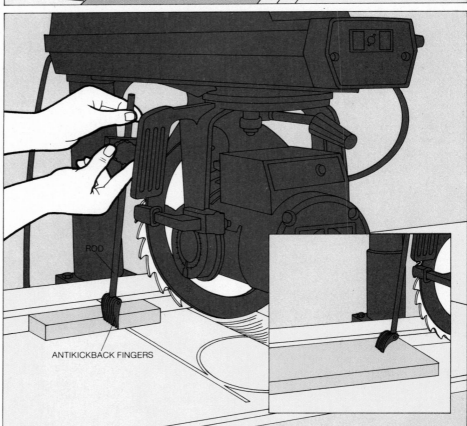

4 Starting the cut. Set the board flat against the fence, on the right side of the table for in-ripping, the left for out-ripping (the drawing at right shows the correct position for an in-rip cut). Turn the saw on and place your hands on the board about 18 inches behind the blade, with one hand next to the fence and the other on the near edge of the board. Slowly push the board into the blade with the hand next to the fence; use your other hand to press the board gently down and toward the fence with your other hand, but not to push.

When your hands are about 6 inches from the blade, move them back along the board and resume the cut. When your hands are on the end of the board and 6 inches from the blade, proceed directly to Step 5.

If the blade binds, shut off the saw and drive an eightpenny cut nail, filed to an oval, through the kerf into the saw table about 2 inches behind the antikickback fingers.

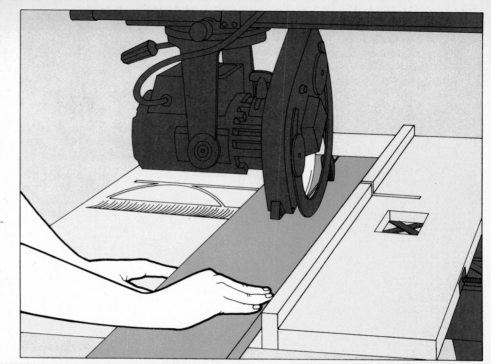

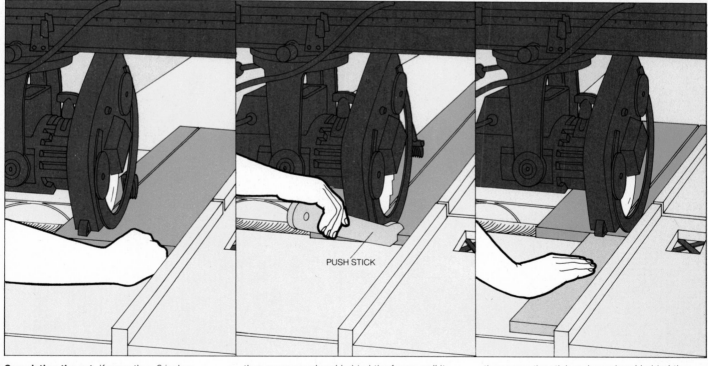

PUSH STICK

5 Completing the cut. If more than 6 inches of the board lie between the blade and the fence, you can complete the cut by hand (*left*). Place the hand nearer the fence at the end of the board, with the thumb tucked under the palm, and take your other hand away from the board. Push the board through the saw, keeping your fingers together and your hand tight against the fence, well away from the blade and guard;

then move your hand behind the fence, pull it back and turn off the motor.

If 1 to 6 inches of the board lie between the blade and the fence, use a push stick (*middle*). Cut a notch at one end of a scrap of 1-inch lumber 16 inches long. Set the notch on the end of the board, centered between the blade and the fence, and push the board through the saw;

then move the stick and your hand behind the fence and pull them back. If the distance between the board and the fence is less than 1 inch (*right*), set a scrap of wood about 16 inches long and 3 inches wide at the end of the board and against the fence. Feed the scrap partway through the saw, cutting the scrap while at the same time pushing the board past the blade, then slide the scrap back along the fence.

The Angle Cuts: Miter, Bevel and Compound

All the myriad angled cuts required in carpentry fall into three basic types. A miter cut, like the one on a rafter end at a roof peak, slants across the face of a board. A bevel cut slants across an edge of a board between opposite faces, as in the top of a gable stud cut to fit the pitch of a roof. And a compound cut, used primarily for finish joints in trim and molding, combines the first two types to provide a board that is mitered across its face and beveled across its edge.

Angle cuts are made with the same tools used for square cuts—the crosscut handsaw, the circular saw, the radial arm saw, and the backsaw and miter box—but the techniques differ somewhat. When using a handsaw to cut an angle, for example, you may want to clamp a guide to the work to prevent the saw from slipping sideways along the board. To start a rough angle cut with a circular saw, you must lift the blade guard; and

since the base plate tilts only as far as 45° in one direction, you must calculate and cut a complementary angle to make a sharper bevel than 45° *(opposite, bottom)*. With the miter box and backsaw—used for the delicate work of cutting trim pieces such as casings, chair rails, baseboards and molding—you must position the wood on edge to make a bevel cut.

For any angle cut with any type of tool, you must take special pains to lay out the work for precision of fit. Generally you can hold one board against another and trace the line of their intersection. In other cases no measurement is needed because the angle is calculated in degrees or is obvious—a 45° miter on window trim, for example. Often, however, you must measure with a protractor and a T bevel—a wooden handle bolted to a pivoted metal blade.

For simple angle cuts, fit a T bevel into an angle you wish to copy, lock the blade

and hold the tool against a board to mark the cut. To set a circular saw for a bevel cut, hold a T bevel against the saw blade—with the saw unplugged—while you adjust the tilt. In situations where it is difficult to align the saw blade by eye but you have a scale on the tool—as in setting a radial arm saw for a bevel cut—use the T bevel to transfer the angle to a scrap of wood, use a protractor to measure it and set the scale of the tool to the measured angle.

The scales on tools are supposed to align exactly with the saw blade, so that a simple setting cuts the angle you want. They rarely do. While the error generally is small—around 1°—it is enough to spoil a visible joint, and it changes as the tool is used. Test periodically to determine the correction needed. And for any angle cut requiring special precision, make a test cut on scrap wood and check the result with a protractor.

Making Miters in Rough Lumber

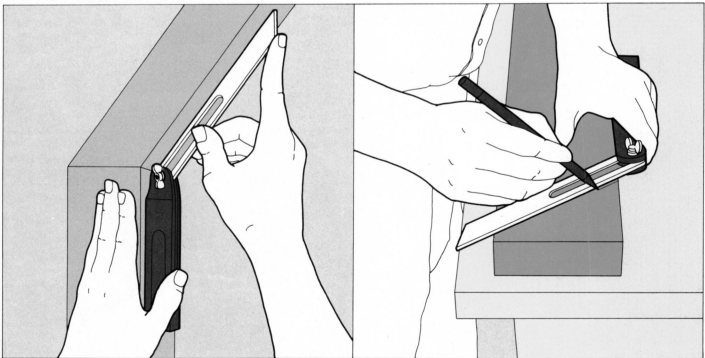

Transferring an angle. Extend the blade of a T bevel and adjust the wing nut on the handle so that the blade moves easily but does not swing free. Fit the T bevel into the angle you plan to transfer *(above, left)* with the blade corre-sponding to the line you are going to cut, and tighten the wing nut. Hold the handle of the T bevel against the edge and the blade across the face of the board to be cut, then mark the cutting line along the blade *(above, right)*.

Cutting an angle with a handsaw. If you are unsure of your ability to follow the cutting line of an angle cut, which is more difficult to start accurately than a straight cut, clamp a piece of scrap—a 2-by-4 will do—to the stock so that it is exactly lined up with the cutting line and overlaps each edge. Begin the cut as you would a square crosscut *(page 15)*. After you have established the kerf, remove the saw from the stock and check to be sure you are following the cutting line. If you are not, restart the kerf.

Cutting an angle with a circular saw. A guide tacked parallel to the cutting mark on the non-waste side of the mark is generally advisable for long cuts and is also helpful on short ones. Rest the base plate of the saw against the guide; then, before turning on the power, lift the blade guard. Hold the guard up as you begin the cut, and release it after it has cleared the edge of the board. Use the guide to keep the blade aligned, but if it strays, start the cut over; do not attempt to force it back on course.

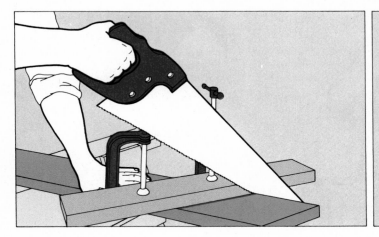

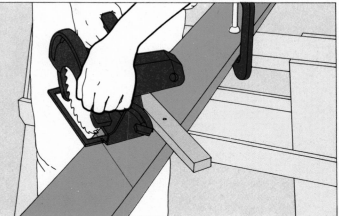

Using a Circular Saw for Bevel and Compound Angles

Setting the blade for a bevel cut. While a handsaw makes this cut quickly if you are adept at cutting to a line—a guide is impractical—the circular saw is far simpler to use. For a bevel no sharper than 45°, set a T bevel to the angle of the cut *(opposite, bottom left)*, then unplug the saw, set its blade for the maximum cutting depth and lay it upside down. Hold the handle of the T bevel firmly against the bottom of the base plate, loosen the protractor nut on the blade-angle scale at the front of the saw, retract the saw guard and tilt the base plate until the blade of the T bevel lies flat against the saw blade. Tighten the protractor nut to secure the setting.

Mark a line square across the board and align the blade with it, using the guide at the front of the base plate. (Check the alignment of the blade and the line carefully by eye; many guides are imprecise.) Start the cut with the guard raised as described for angle cuts *(above, right)*.

For a bevel sharper than 45° in construction lumber, use a protractor to set the T bevel to the complement of the angle desired, then use the T bevel to set the saw blade as described above. For sharp bevels in shaped boards, such as trim, use a miter box *(overleaf)*.

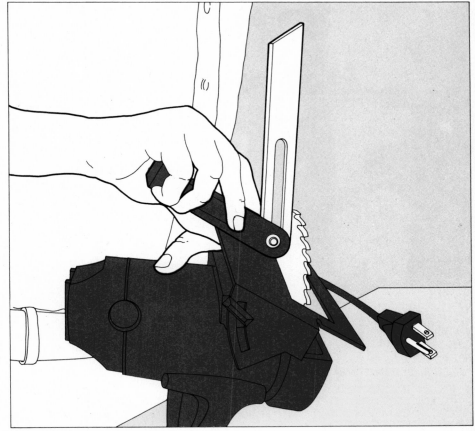

Making a compound cut. With a handsaw, this two-directional cut generally requires two separate operations—a simple angle cut followed by a bevel cut. With a circular saw it is done in a single pass. Lay out the simple angle, then set the saw blade for the bevel (*page 29, bottom*), but follow the cutting procedure that is used for a simple angle (*page 29, top right*).

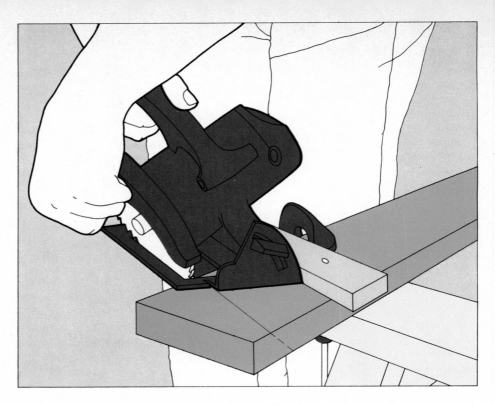

Cutting Trim with a Miter Box

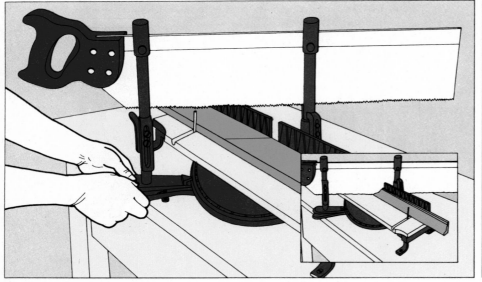

STOP BLOCK

Making simple angle or bevel cuts. Set the saw angle desired, correcting for scale error if necessary. For a simple angle cut, place the board flat side down in the box and secure it in position—using miter-box clamps or woodworking clamps—so the saw will cut on the waste side of the mark. Lower the saw and make the cut.

Follow the same procedure for a bevel cut, but place the board on edge, with its flat side against the back of the miter box (*inset*).

Making a cut sharper than 45°. Measure and mark the angle to be cut and place the marked stock in the miter box. Move the saw blade as close to the cutting line as possible, then shift the stock to align the cutting line with the blade.

Fit a block of scrap wood between the back of the miter box and the stock and clamp the block in place. Hold the stock firmly while you make the cut, checking constantly to see that the cutting line does not stray from the plane of the saw.

A Radial Arm Saw for Speed and Precision

Setting the saw for simple angle cuts. For a right-hand angle cut, loosen the miter lock and swing the arm to the right, setting the indicator on the miter scale to the angle you will cut, correcting for scale error if necessary. On a typical radial arm saw, the arm will lock automatically at 45°, and you must release the lock to move it. Mark the stock and brace it against the fence with your left hand, positioning it so that the blade will cut on the waste side of the mark; use your right hand to pull the saw through the board. If precision is important, make a test cut on scrap.

To cut a left-hand miter in a flat board, flip the board upside down and use the right-hand miter position. If the board surface is shaped and will not lie flat when you flip it, move the fence to its rear position and swing the saw to the left to lock it in the left-hand miter position *(inset)*. Use a supplementary worktable, if necessary, to support the wood, and pull the saw through the board with your left hand.

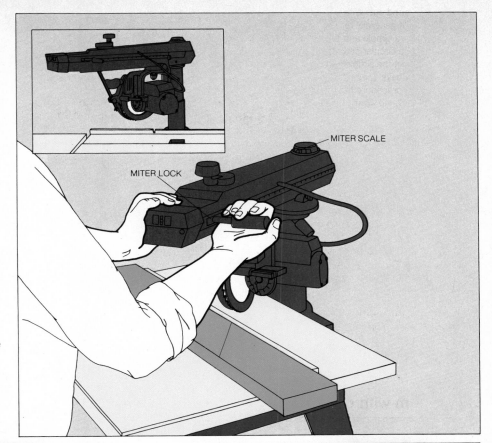

MITER SCALE

MITER LOCK

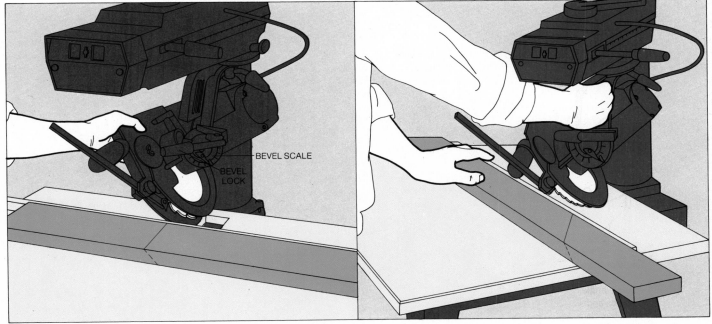

BEVEL SCALE

BEVEL LOCK

Making bevel and compound cuts. For a bevel cut, raise the arm of the saw until the blade clears the table by about 3 inches; release the bevel lock and tilt the blade counterclockwise to the correct degree reading on the bevel scale, then retighten the bevel lock *(left)*. Make sure that the saw guard has enough play so that it will not jam when you move the saw; if necessary, clear the guard of sawdust and lubricate it. (If the guard jams while you are pulling the saw, stop the saw immediately and free the guard.) Use your right hand to position and steady the wood, and your left hand to pull the saw. Make a test cut to check accuracy. For a compound cut, set both the miter and the bevel scales. The cutting procedure follows that used for a bevel cut, but you must switch hand positions if the saw is set for a right-hand miter *(right)*.

Masterpieces of the Woodworker

"Wood," wrote William Penn three centuries ago, "is a substance with a soul." Anybody who has ever worked with wood, who has come to appreciate the distinct personalities of oak and walnut, of pine and chestnut and cedar, would almost certainly have to agree. For warmth of color and texture, for unique patterning, for resilience and strength coupled with responsiveness to tools, there never has been another building material to rival it.

These qualities have been exploited over the centuries in many ways, as can be seen in the old and new examples of the woodworker's art on the following pages. Structural elements are deliberately left exposed to become part of the interior design of a room. Elsewhere wood is used purely for esthetic effect, as decoration. In still other homes, function and esthetics are combined in beautifully worked paneling, doors and railings.

Fortunately, throughout most of history, wood of all sorts has been in abundant supply. Prime woods, the likes of which are seldom seen in lumberyards today, once were used almost as casually as No. 2 Common is today. Such profligacy is no longer possible or desirable as select woods have become luxuries. But where wood can be celebrated—in paneling, in trim, in doors and in exposed structural members—craftsmen continue to delight in its timeless virtues, selecting the species to use for its particular combination of qualities.

Oak is prized for strength and durability, pine and fir for workability. A rustic interior wants exposed wood with a rough, strong grain, such as chestnut; mahogany and walnut have the sort of subtle grain that harmonize with a highly polished room. And where pronounced wood patterning or color is to play a major role in the effect you are after, it will certainly pay to hand-select lumber, board by board.

Some craftsmen want such subtle effects that they draft their final design only after they have the wood in hand and have studied it thoroughly. Charles and Henry Greene, the brother architects whose 1909 interior is shown on page 38, top, designed the carved friezes with motifs of stylized branches in order to emphasize the grain of the individual pieces of mahogany.

Other woodworkers may find the simplest, plainest treatment of wood—without carving, staining or any other civilizing refinements—the most congenial. It all depends upon the nature of the room and the instincts of the craftsman.

A wealth of woodwork. A two-story entrance well provides a stunning glimpse of exposed, warm-toned wood in paneling, cornices, moldings, railings and rafters. In this yet-to-be-finished Connecticut residence, the builder-designers have incorporated touches of Victorian whimsy and grace, using old pine balusters, for example, and new door and window trim that has been hand-carved in the old manner. The round window, designed to be fitted with stained glass, is framed, barrel-style, in 6-inch strips of red cedar—one piece at center right is yet to be nailed. Cedar also frames the balcony enclosure and the diagonally paneled ceiling and walls.

Posts, Beams and Rafters
Too Beautiful to Hide

Framing members, particularly if hand-hewn of gracefully aged wood, add architectural muscle and sinew to an interior just by being visible. In colonial times, such an honest expression of the builder's art was often a matter of necessity, since plaster and paint were hard to get.

As the colonies grew more prosperous, the chestnut, oak and pine that formed the rugged frames of houses were covered up. To the modern eye, however, such elements are freshly perceived as worthy of display for their surface texture and for the stark logic of their forms. The restoration of an old house is often an opportunity to reveal long-buried timbers. In constructing new houses, the designer may choose to recycle timbers from torn-down buildings, or use new wood of suitable character.

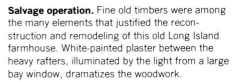

Apotheosis of a cow barn. The Great Hall of Packwood House, Warwickshire, England, began life in the 17th Century as a farm building, but its handsome oak "crucks," or curved roof rafters, inspired the owners to convert the space into a residence in the 1920s.

Salvage operation. Fine old timbers were among the many elements that justified the reconstruction and remodeling of this old Long Island farmhouse. White-painted plaster between the heavy rafters, illuminated by the light from a large bay window, dramatizes the woodwork.

34

Rustic ceiling. In a Vermont hay barn-turned-modern house, hundred-year-old oak rafters and board roof sheathing are preserved intact as the ceiling, a counterpoint for sleekly elegant plaster walls. The rich toast color of the antique wood was brought up with sandblasting. A layer of insulation plus an outer roof were added over the old for weathertightness.

Modern geometry. Constructed with all new materials, this Connecticut country house borrows from the past in using rough-sawn beams and leaving some of them visible in this second-story living room. Their warmly weathered color was intensified during construction by 8 to 10 weeks' exposure to the elements.

Purely, Purposively Decorative

Ornamental woodwork often is passed over as unaffordable nowadays, but it once played a major part in interior finishing. Every era had its own finials, moldings and fretwork, and a craftsman had to execute them in the right combinations and proportions. Such work still has a place, as part of an authentic reproduction or for its own eye-pleasing sake.

Gothic fantasies. Book niches, framed with filigreed wooden arches, are among the experiments in Gothic Revival style at Horace Walpole's 18th Century English villa, Strawberry Hill. A medieval church screen inspired the arches.

Classical craftsmanship. Designs of Roman antiquity, adapted in Renaissance Italy and re-adapted in colonial America, provide the patterns for this extravagantly detailed parlor in 18th Century Gunston Hall, Virginia.

Triumphal arch. What was once the molded
pine frame of a pair of massive sliding doors has
been preserved as freestanding sculpture in
this remodeling of a late-Victorian house on Long
Island. The open doorway maintains the sense
of two distinct living spaces provided by the solid
walls of the original floor plan, but without
the drawbacks of restricted light and movement.

Form and Function Joined

When decorative woodworking is linked with functional elements, the results can be even greater than the sum of the parts.

Customarily, such unions have been consummated in decorative railings, in carved posts and beams, in elaborate doors and in wall and ceiling paneling. Though all of these continue to be used, paneling is perhaps the most frequently revived feature. It offers the broadest canvas for displaying the subtleties of wood grain, color and texture, whether it simply covers wall and ceiling surfaces, as in the examples below, or also becomes part of built-in furniture, as at right.

A delight in wood. Teak planks, gently rounded at the edges, oiled, and pegged with end-grain teak, reflect a silky, sensuous glow in the living room of a 1909 Greene Brothers house, which has beams, walls and furniture of wood.

A rustic retreat. Taking its form and finishing inspiration from chalet construction, this Adirondack vacation house has interior walls and pitched ceiling sheathed in unfinished spruce. Darker floors are fir; stairs and trim are cherry.

Wood for warmth. Waxed cedar wraps the interior of a Colorado ski house in lively reds and browns to accent the gray of slate and stone. Vertical planks, which catch the sun, are rough-hewn, those overhead are polished smooth.

Motifs in marquetry. A four-paneled folding door, put together in intricate patterns of teak diamonds within diamonds, screens the dining room from the two-story living room of a modern villa in Sicily. On the reverse side of the door, the same pattern fits into a towering wall of teak planking, most of it set vertically but interrupted with two smaller diamond insets. The window has small glass panes in deep mullions to help screen out the high sun of the Sicilian summer.

Flights of Fancy

The staircase, with its enormous potential for architectural drama, naturally invites the designer's imagination; few parts of a house provide such opportunities for converting a utilitarian structure into a major element of design.

When stairs are constructed of wood, which lends itself so beautifully to ornamentation, they permit the virtuoso exercise of talent in carving, bending, turning and inlay to embellish the various parts—from treads and risers to stringers, balusters, railings, newel posts, landings and paneling—that go to make up the functioning whole.

Renaissance and Baroque staircases had straight, muscular runs and closed stringers. From the mid-18th Century on, however, open stringers, their surfaces richly ornamented, were fitted with delicate balusters and graceful rails.

Curved stairs were also tried—some "flying" with a daring lack of visible support—but not until the advent of iron posts have freestanding wooden "snails," like that below, been possible.

Diagonal thrust. A massive wooden archway frames the grand stair of Carter's Grove in Virginia. A superb example of the Colonial Georgian style, it has fine detailing that includes walnut nosings on the edges of the pine treads, nail-hiding plugs hand-carved in the shape of fleurs-de-lis, elaborately turned balusters, spiraled newels and beveled yellow-pine paneling.

A helix for a balustrade. Complementing the vaulted ceiling of this restored 1609 hunting lodge in Tuscany is a modern spiral stair with steps of travertine marble cantilevered from a central iron post and wrapped by a balustrade of chestnut-veneered pine. The pine core was curved by steaming. Thin chestnut strips 9 feet long were then bent and glued to the pine in alternating bands 4 inches and 8 inches wide.

A Library for Carpenters

Unlike some other crafts of home repair and improvement, woodworking has inspired a literature remarkable for its depth and variety. One of the earliest works in the English language on the subject, *Mechanick Exercise,* was published in 1677, and some books put out a century or more ago, such as Thomas Tredgold's 1840 *Elementary Principles of Carpentry (below),* are readable today. New books for amateurs and professionals continue to be issued in a flood: the Library of Congress indexes 110 under "Woodworking—Amateurs' Manuals," one of many classifications related to woodworking.

The selected list on this page samples the variety while emphasizing works related to home building and repair rather than cabinetmaking. It includes some books meant for pleasure and background—such as the beautifully illustrated descriptions of old tools and techniques by the noted artist Eric Sloane—as well as guides for the amateur, professional monographs, formal textbooks and technical compilations.

MODERN TECHNICAL

☐ BASIC CONSTRUCTION TECHNIQUES FOR HOUSES AND SMALL BUILDINGS SIMPLY EXPLAINED, prepared by U.S. Navy Bureau of Naval Personnel. Dover Publications Inc., New York, 1972. A nononsense manual covering all facets of home construction from planning to painting, it includes seven chapters on carpentry and woodworking. A spartan but readable and practical reference.

☐ CABINETMAKING AND MILLWORK, by John L. Feirer. Chas. A. Bennett Co. Inc., Peoria, Ill., 1970. More than a reference work on cabinetmaking, this book includes detailed chapters on materials, design, tools and machinery, construction and finishing. Although this definitive book has more than 900 pages, a good index keeps it manageable.

☐ CARPENTRY FOR BEGINNERS, by Charles H. Hayward. Emerson Books Inc., New York, 1969. This beginner's text, one of many books by a well-known craftsman-writer, describes the basics of carpentry, such as measuring, marking, nailing, gluing and joining.

☐ THE COMPLETE BOOK OF POWER TOOLS, by R. J. De Cristoforo. Harper and Row, New York, 1972. The classic explanation of the use of the power tools that are designed for home workshops. Clearly illustrated.

☐ CONSTRUCTION PRINCIPLES, MATERIALS & METHODS by Harold B. Olin. Printers and Publishers Inc., Danville, Ill., 1975. A massive volume, written for professionals, on home construction materials and techniques. It presents a staggering display of information, including sections on asphalt, plastics and wiring as well as many chapters on wood products and construction methods. Many charts, tables and diagrams.

☐ A DICTIONARY OF TOOLS USED IN WOODWORKING AND THE ALLIED TRADES C. 1700-1970, by R. A. Salaman. Allen & Unwin, London, 1975. A catalogue of thousands of hand tools with brief descriptions of their uses. Invaluable for a tool collector and useful to amateur woodworkers.

☐ FINE WOODWORKING TECHNIQUES, by the editors of *Fine Woodworking* magazine. Taunton Press, Newton, Conn., 1978. A collection of 50 articles by craftsmen who have contributed to this bimonthly magazine. Articles focus on specific woodworking problems, techniques and tools.

☐ MODERN WOODWORKING, by Willis Wagner. Goodheart-Willcox Co., South Holland, Ill., 1974. A textbook that is widely used in secondary-school shop courses, this well-illustrated book provides the technical information needed in general carpentry.

☐ THE USE OF HAND WOODWORKING TOOLS, by Leo P. McDonnell. Van Nostrand Reinhold Co., New York, 1978. Primarily a tool book that explains standard techniques. Designed as a high-school textbook, it is easy to understand.

☐ WHAT WOOD IS THAT?, by Herbert L. Edlin. The Viking Press, New York, 1969. After a brief discussion of the historical uses for wood, the steps for identification of 40 commonly used woods are set forth by 14 key characteristics, such as color, grain, weight and hardness. Wafer-thin samples of the woods are provided on the inside cover.

TRADITIONAL

☐ A MUSEUM OF EARLY AMERICAN TOOLS, by Eric Sloane. Wilfred Funk Inc., New York, 1964. Beautifully illustrated by the author, brief but informative essays describe the uses and lore of colonial American tools.

☐ COUNTRY FURNITURE, by Aldren A. Watson. Thomas Y. Crowell Co., New York, 1974. An intriguing account of the life style, tools and craftsmanship of early American furniture makers. Illustrated by the author, the book contains excerpts from 16th and 17th Century journals, account books and letters.

☐ OLD WAYS OF WORKING WITH WOOD, by Alex W. Bealer. Barre Publishing Co., Barre, Mass., fourth edition, 1977. From felling a tree to turning wood on a foot-powered lathe, the techniques of pre-industrial America provide perspective on those of today.

☐ A REVERENCE FOR WOOD, by Eric Sloane. Wilfred Funk Inc., New York, 1965; Ballantine Books (paper), New York, 1973. Pen-and-ink sketches by the author show time-honored methods for cutting, shaping and joining pieces of wood. The text uses the tools and techniques illustrated as a vehicle to relate a chronicle of daily life in early America.

VINTAGE

☐ CARPENTRY CRAFT PROBLEMS, by H. H. Siegele. Frederick J. Drake & Co., 1942; reprinted by Craftsman Books, Solana Beach, Calif., 1975. Fundamentals of carpentry, from using a steel square to framing and raising a wall.

☐ ELEMENTARY PRINCIPLES OF CARPENTRY, by Thomas Tredgold. John Weales, London, 1840. Well worth a search through the library, this venerable tome includes research on timber, floor construction, domes and stressing beams. Its 50 engravings include a sketch of the roof beams in "the juvenile prison in Parkhurst on the Ile of Wight."

☐ JOINERY AND CARPENTRY, edited by Richard Greenhalgh. Sir Isaac Pitman & Sons Ltd., London, 1929. Six volumes. A vintage series with engravings and photographs illustrating a broad range of topics including tool selection, and stairway and partition construction.

Panels: Awkward Sizes and Difficult Materials

Much carpentry today requires the cutting of large, awkward and refractory panels. Subflooring, roof sheathing and cupboards are now made almost always of plywood or particleboard, and commonly used interior doors are covered with particleboard (even paneled doors are of particleboard with molded panels).

Panels are difficult to cut partly because of their size but also because of their composition. The glues and binders that hold together the veneer layers of plywood or the chopped-up wood in particleboard quickly dull saw blades.

The big problem, however, is size. To hold clumsily large pieces, you need a firm work surface; to make a long cut straight, you need a guide.

Two sturdy sawhorses alone provide support when crosscutting with a circular saw, but ripping requires additional stiffeners—two 2-by-4s that prevent the pan-el from sagging as the saw passes along the panel's midsection. With a radial arm saw, use two outrigger tables bolted to the floor; smooth tops reduce friction as the panels move past the blade. A third outrigger table helps when cutting many panels—it supports the waste piece and lets one person do the entire job.

Straightedge guides are equally important. A radial arm saw already has one—the fence—that is convenient for ripping, but needs the help of two others, made of scrap, for large crosscutting jobs. You can make a guide for a circular saw, using the perfectly square factory-cut edge of a piece of particleboard. A two-piece, permanent jig is best for repeated crosscuts; a one-piece jig, assembled for a single job, is sufficient for ripping.

For smoothness as well as straightness of cut, the blade you choose is important. Standard rip and crosscut blades dull quickly. A carbide-tipped combination blade will stand up longer to the materials in plywood and particleboard, but it will give a relatively rough cut. A special plywood blade will give a cleaner, smoother cut but will dull faster than the carbide-tipped combination.

If you own a radial arm saw, use it for panel cutting when you can do the job conveniently in your workshop. Its built-in straightedge, the fence, is easily adapted to production work. It will crosscut up to 48 inches if you adapt the saw *(pages 44-45)*. You can rip widths from 14 to 24 inches with the saw in the out-rip position *(page 45, bottom)*. And if the piece to be ripped from the panel is wider than this, simply measure the piece you need, subtract that measurement plus the kerf width from the width of the panel and set the saw up for an in-rip cut *(pages 25-27, Steps 1 through 5)*.

A Homemade Guide for Crosscuts

1 **Assembling the jig.** Screw together two 4-foot lengths of ¾-inch particleboard, one of the pieces 12 inches wide and the other 4 inches wide, cut from an end of the panel that has an unmarred factory-cut edge. Align the two pieces so that the factory-cut edge of the narrow piece faces into the middle of the wide piece.

2 **Trimming the jig.** Clamp the jig to the bench top so that at least 6 inches of the wide board extends over the bench edge. Set the base plate of the saw against the factory-cut edge of the narrow piece, and saw through the wide piece along its entire length. The edge of the narrow piece thus becomes a guide to position the saw blade at the edge of the wide piece—the jig's cutting edge. Varnish the jig to reduce warping.

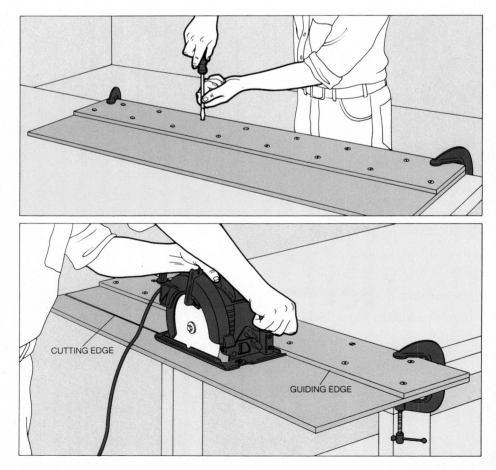

CUTTING EDGE

GUIDING EDGE

3 **Cutting the panel.** Align the cutting edge of the jig base with marks for the amount to be cut off, clamp the jig to the panel and then, using the cutting edge of the jig as a guide, score the panel with a utility knife or, to prevent gouging the jig, a chisel held bevel side out *(page 95, Step 5)* but tilted toward you.

Set the blade depth to account for the thickness of the jig base as well as that of the panel to be cut, position the base plate against the guiding edge of the jig as in Step 2, and then saw through the panel, using the crosscutting technique described on page 16, Steps 1 and 2.

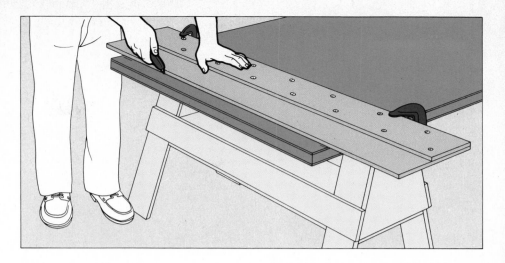

Making Clean Cuts with the Grain

1 **Building a work surface.** Set two sawhorses at a distance 2 feet shorter than the length of the panel to be cut. Nail two 2-by-4s as long as the panel to the sawhorses, keeping the 2-by-4s parallel and about 3 feet apart.

2 **Positioning the jig.** Mark both panel ends for the amount to be cut off, make a second pair of marks further into the panel a distance equal to the distance between the saw blade and the base plate's left side; then clamp to the panel at the second pair of marks a piece of ¾-inch particleboard that is 10 inches wide by 8 feet long and has been cut to leave a factory-made edge as a base-plate guide. At three places along the midsection of this jig, check that the jig edge and the panel edge are the same distance apart as at the ends; at these places nail the jig to the panel. Cut the panel following the technique described in Step 3, above.

If the plywood panel has been previously cut, its edge may be bowed or out of square. In this case, use a string to check alignment of your jig.

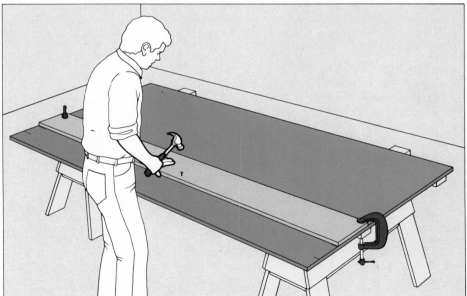

Crosscutting Panels with a Radial Arm Saw

1 Expanding the work surface. Move the fence closer to the arm's support post by loosening the clamps behind the table and sliding the spacer boards toward you. Position the fence between the clamps and the spacer boards and tighten the clamps. At the sides of the saw, set up worktables that are at least 26 inches wide and the same height as the saw table.

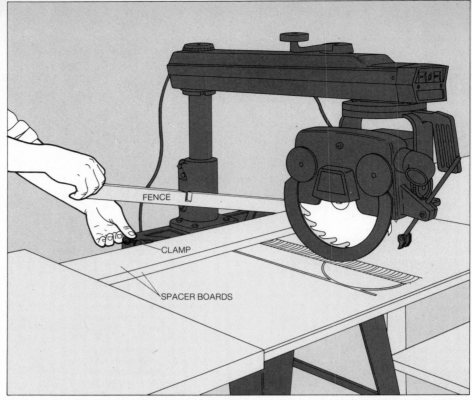

FENCE

CLAMP

SPACER BOARDS

2 Setting up a large crosscut. At the rear of the arm, raise the saw and turn the yoke 180° so that the teeth of the blade face you, then lock it in position. Mark the panel for the cut and align the mark with the blade. At both ends of the panel, fasten 24-inch straightedges to the worktables and then pull the panel back 12 inches. Lower the saw, start the motor and slowly feed the panel into the blade until the far panel edge hits the fence. Unlock the motor and pull the saw toward you until it reaches the end of the arm. Lock the saw in position while the motor is operating.

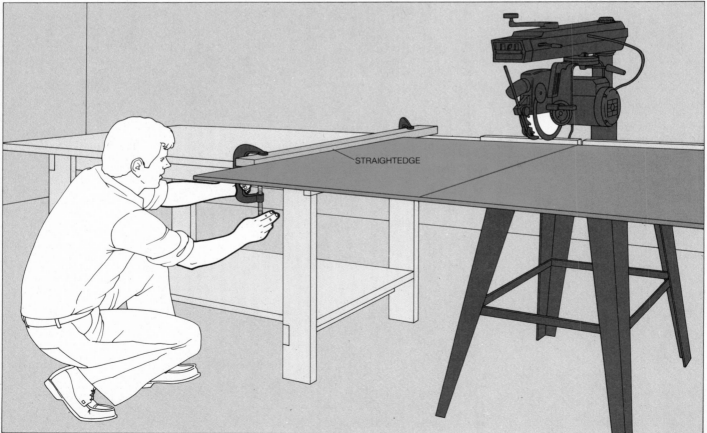

STRAIGHTEDGE

3 **Extending the cut.** With the saw still operating, place your hands under the panel and, keeping pressure against the fence, slowly lift the
panel, cutting it farther, until it hits the bottom of
the motor. Lower the panel to the table, unlock the saw and push it back to the rear of the
arm. Now turn it off and lock it in place.

With a helper, turn the panel over and place it
on the table between the straightedges with the
far edge several inches in front of the blade.
Start the saw and again slide the panel into the
blade until the far edge hits the fence. Then
unlock the motor and pull the saw toward you as
before to complete the cut across the panel.

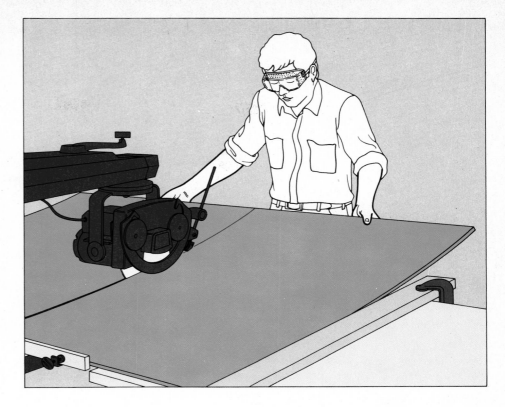

Using the Saw
for Long Rip Cuts

Beginning the cut. With the fence in the back
position (*opposite, Step 1*), turn the saw to the
out-rip position (blade parallel to the fence,
motor between blade and fence). Set the panel to
the left of the saw with the leading edge
against the fence, align the blade with the cutting
line on the panel end and lock the motor in
place. Adjust the blade guard and antikickback
fingers (*page 26, Steps 2 and 3*), start the motor and, with your left hand on the back of the
panel and your right keeping pressure against
the fence, feed the panel into the blade.

After the blade has made a kerf about 1 foot
long, you may have to turn off the saw and drive a
nail through the kerf into the table surface to
keep the blade from binding (*page 27, Step 4*).
Restart the motor and continue feeding the
panel toward the blade. If you are working with a
helper, do not have him take hold of the waste
piece until it is two thirds of the way past the
blade; from that point on, have him merely
support the wood and not pull it. Finish the cut as
you would for in-ripping (*page 27, Step 5*).

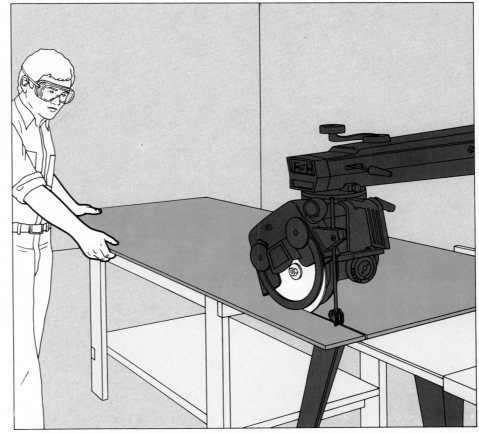

The Tricks of Putting Curves into Wood

The basic frame of a house fits together along straight lines, but much of the finish carpentry involves curves, trickier to cut. Some of the curved cuts are utilitarian—for example, in holes through walls, floors and roof for pipes or ducts. Others—the scalloped trim of a porch, the arch of an elegant door or the curve of a circular window—are decorative.

Whatever the curve's purpose, it requires tools and techniques different from those used for straight cuts. For most curves the best tool is an electric saber saw, ideally one with variable-speed control. Blades ¼ inch wide with 8 to 10 points per inch are suitable for most jobs, but other blades are available for special uses: a hollow-ground blade, for example, will make splinter-free cuts in plywood; a blade with 12 or 14 points per inch is advisable for scrollwork.

When power is not available or when work space is too cramped for a saber saw, turn to any of several handsaws designed specifically for cutting curves. A coping saw has a delicate blade and a limited cutting range; it is best suited to finish joints in woodwork and to fine,

intricate scrollwork. The keyhole saw can tackle heavier tasks, while the compass saw serves for still rougher work. Both come with an assortment of blades designed for different materials. The blades are tapered, with narrow tips for turns and for cutouts started from small drilled holes; and because the blades can be reversed, compass and keyhole saws are ideal for use in jobs with tight clearances and awkward undercuts.

Since you must guide all of these saws freehand, it is essential to mark a guideline before cutting any curve. More often than not, you can simply hold an object to be duplicated—a section of decorative trim or a window sash, perhaps—in place and trace its outline. But some situations demand more complex calculations and marking techniques. For instance, to mark an elliptical hole for a round pipe passing through the roof, you must plot the pitch of the roof and the size of the pipe on cardboard, then cut out the marked cardboard as a template to transfer the ellipse to the roof *(pages 49-50).*

In other situations you must resort to scribing, a marking technique for fitting

material to an existing curve. Generally it consists of setting the wood—the floor boards in a semicircular alcove, for instance—against the curve and running a simple school compass around the curve to duplicate, or scribe, the arc on the boards *(page 47).* If you are scribing overlapping boards, as when you fit siding around a circular opening *(page 48),* you must position the work carefully and set the compass to the exact distance that will provide the overlap. And for some jobs, such as the cutting of a curved casing for an archway, you must combine template-making and scribing.

When you cut a curve, be especially careful of the pressure you apply; under excess pressure, a handsaw blade will buckle and a saber-saw blade may shoot out of the cut or snap in two. Mark the guidelines for a saber saw on the unfinished side of the board if possible, because the upstroke cut of the blade splinters the wood; if you must work on the finished side, cover the guidelines with transparent tape to minimize the damage. Steady the board by clamping it to a worktable or setting it on sawhorses.

Sawing an Irregular Outline

Cutting an interior curve with a handsaw. Drill a ¾-inch starter hole through the waste area, insert the tip of the saw blade—in this example, a keyhole saw—and make a few short, vertical strokes to start the cut. Then lower the blade to a 45° angle and follow the curved guideline with long, even strokes and light pressure—too much pressure on the blade will bend or buckle it. To saw around sharp turns use short strokes, made with the narrow tip of the blade.

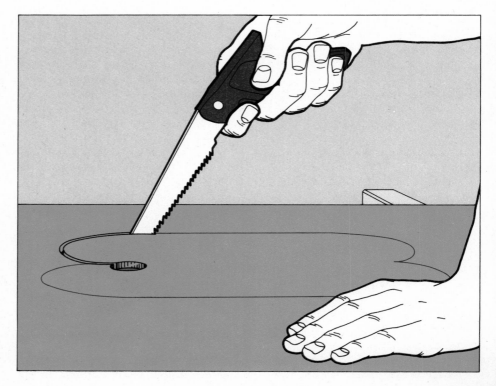

Cutting with a saber saw. Pressing the saw down and forward, and keeping the base plate flat against the wood, follow the broad curves of a pattern. Bypass any sharp turns—forcing the saw or pushing it sideways for these curves will damage the blade. When you have cut the waste wood away from the broad curves, go back to the sharper angles. On a tight curve, where the saw blade is likely to bind, make radial cuts in the waste area, then saw along the outline. The waste will drop off in pieces as you saw, giving the blade more room to turn (*inset*).

A plunge cut for an interior curve. With the saw motor off and the blade clear of the wood, rest the front edge, or toe, of the base plate on the waste area near the marked guideline. Turn the motor on and, pressing firmly on the base-plate toe, slowly lower the back of the saw until the blade touches and cuts through the wood. When the base plate rests flat on the wood, saw to the guideline and cut in the normal fashion.

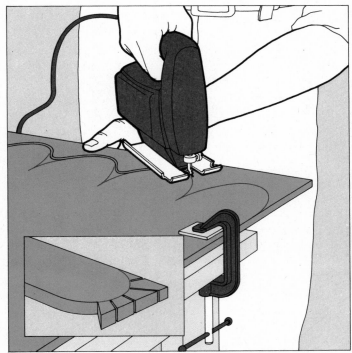

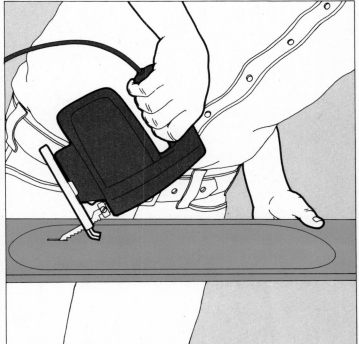

Scribing a Gentle Arc

Copying a curve with a compass. Butt the material against the curve it must fit—in this example the material is floorboards, the curve is that of an alcove wall—and set the legs of a compass to a distance slightly greater than the widest gap between the curve and the edges of the boards. Keeping the plane of the legs at a right angle to the surface you are marking, and in a line that is at a right angle to the curve, move the compass point around the curve so that the pencil point marks a corresponding curve on the boards.

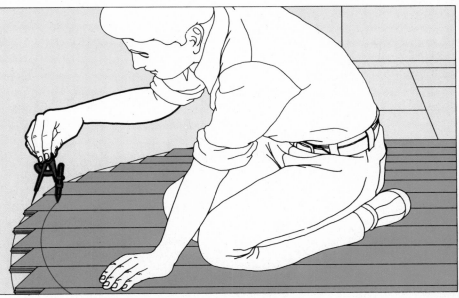

Fitting Siding to a Curve

1 **The bottom board.** To fit clapboard siding around the curve of a circular window frame, you must scribe and cut a series of arcs on the clapboards. Tack the first board to be cut directly over the last complete board below the frame, add the width of the siding overlap to the distance between the bottom of the frame and the top of the tacked board, and subtract the total from the width of the board. Set the legs of a compass to this distance and use the compass to scribe an arc on the tacked board. Take the marked board down, cut the curve and install the board at the bottom of the frame.

2 **The side boards.** Tack a side board at its correct level and about 2 inches from the frame, set the legs of a compass as you would for simple scribing (*page 47*), and scribe the arc on the board. Mark, cut and install all the side boards before starting the final step of the job.

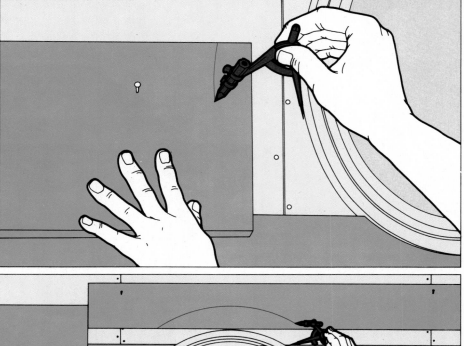

3 **The top board.** Above the frame, tack a board perfectly level, with its bottom edge resting on the frame. Set the compass legs to the width of the siding overlap plus the distance between the last side board and the tacked board, and move the compass point along the top of the frame to scribe the final arc.

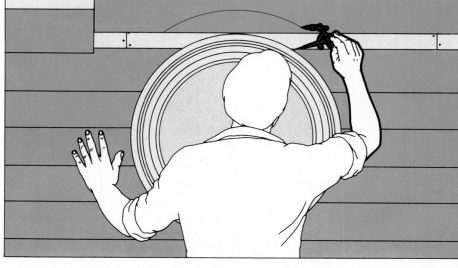

How to Mark an Oval

1 Finding the axes. To plan an elliptical hole for a cylinder passing through a sloping plane—typically, a cylindrical vent or stovepipe passing through a roof—first find the axes of the ellipse by the following method. On a large piece of cardboard, draw a horizontal and a sloped line at the exact angle of the roof pitch. In any section of the horizontal line, mark off the diameter of the pipe plus any required clearance; then draw perpendicular lines from the marks to intersect the sloped line.

From the intersection points, extend two more lines perpendicular to the sloped line, mark off the pipe diameter plus clearance on these lines, and connect the marks to form a rectangle with its base on the sloped line. Finally, draw two lines bisecting the four sides of the rectangle. The longer line is the major axis of the ellipse; the shorter one is the minor axis.

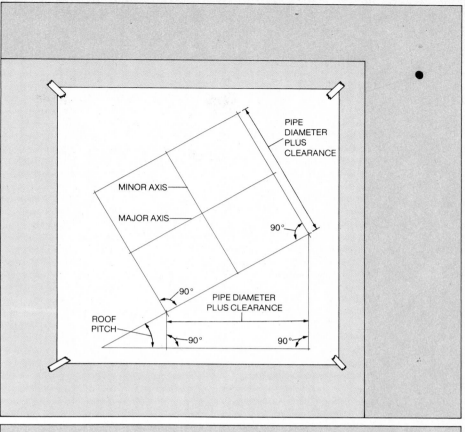

2 Finding the focuses. Set the legs of a compass to half the length of the major axis; place the point of the compass at either end of the minor axis and swing the pencil in an arc that intersects the major axis at two points. These points are the focuses of the ellipse.

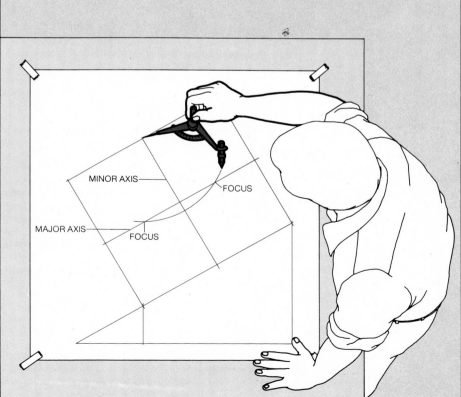

3 **Drawing the ellipse.** Set the cardboard on a piece of scrap wood and drive nails partway into the wood through the focuses and at one end of the minor axis. Tie a string tightly around the three nails; then replace the nail on the axis with a pencil and, keeping the string taut, swing the pencil around to outline the ellipse. Cut out the cardboard ellipse as a template for transferring the curve to the roof.

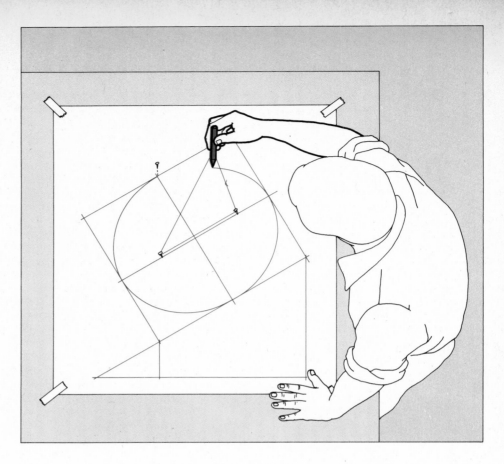

Tracing an Archway

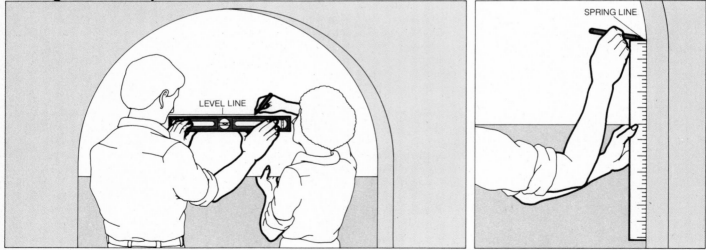

1 **Transferring the curve to paper.** To cut a large arc from straight boards, as in the casing for an arched doorway or window opening, make a set of templates. First tape a piece of paper over the arc and outline the entire curve on the paper. Have a helper hold a level against the paper within 2 feet of the top of the arc, and mark a level line across the paper.

2 **Finding the spring line.** If the curved part of the casing joins a straight section, as in an arch, move a straightedge up and down against the straight section and mark the paper at the highest spot where no space can be seen between the straightedge and the straight section. This marks the spring line, where the curve of the arc begins. Mark the spring line on the other side of the arch, then lay the paper on the floor.

3 **Scribing the template.** Set the legs of a compass to the width of the pieces you will cut—generally, the casing width—and run the point along the marked arc to scribe a second arc above it. From the center of the level line, draw a perpendicular line up through the double arc.

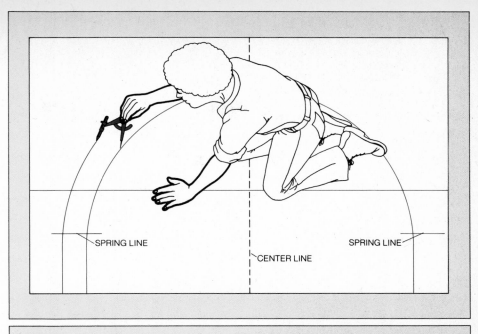

4 **Dividing the template.** At the top of the double arc, draw a line perpendicular to the center line and parallel to the level line below. Along this top line, set the top edge of the board you will cut; on the template paper draw a line along the bottom edge of the board to intersect the double arc on both sides. This second line marks the divisions between the top and side templates.

To complete the side templates, draw lines across the double arc about 5 inches below each of the spring lines and parallel to the level line. These lines mark the butt joints at the bottoms of the two side templates. Cut the paper at both curves, at the division lines and at the butt joints, making three sections. Tack them to boards (*inset*), and trace their outlines as guidelines.

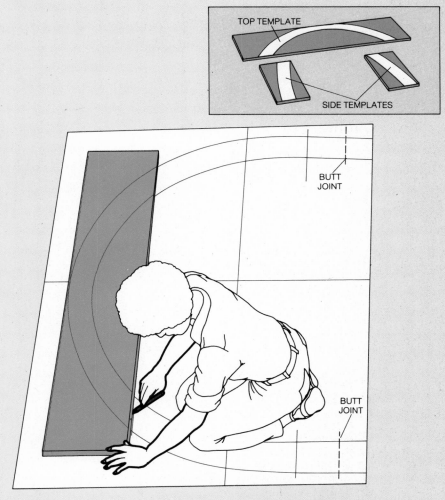

Table Saw and Band Saw—Handy Extras

House carpentry rarely calls for stationary power tools—the radial arm saw is the only one that is discussed in detail in this chapter. But two other types of stationary saw, the table saw and the band saw, are common in home workshops. Neither of these can offer the combination of versatility and accuracy that distinguishes the radial arm saw, but if you have either tool, you may want to consider using it for some cutting jobs.

A table saw consists essentially of a power-driven circular blade that projects through a slot in a metal worktable (the safety guard that always covers the blade has been omitted for clarity in the pictures below and opposite, top). The saw has an adjustable rip fence and a completely unobstructed space around its blade so that it can make rip cuts in long boards. However, because the wood must be moved past the blade, large panels are troublesome to handle. A second fence, which is set at an angle to the blade with a miter gauge, is used to push boards past the blade for crosscuts and miter cuts, and a crank or lever tilts the blade for bevel cuts.

On the band saw the blade is exactly what the name implies—a continuous steel band. It runs in tracks on an upper and a lower wheel, and is covered at the wheels by guards and at the rear of the saw by a throat, or vertical arm, so that only the section above the worktable is exposed. Using a thin, flexible blade—as narrow as ⅛ inch—you can pivot the wood freehand for precise curves. With stronger, wider blades—the maximum width is generally 1½ inches—you can take advantage of the saw's great depth of cut (up to 6 inches on the majority of models) to make straight cuts on very thick lumber or to slice a thick board into thinner ones.

Both types of saw call for careful planning and adjustments. On the table saw you must adjust the blade height so that the teeth will protrude about ⅛ inch above the surface of the wood you are cutting. For an accurate rip cut you must set the rip fence to an exact distance from the blade (if the tips of the saw teeth are alternately slanted left and right, measure from a tooth that slants in the direction of the fence).

For an angle cut you will need to slide the miter gauge into a slot to the left or right of the blade (carpenters prefer the left slot for the majority of cuts), set the gauge to the desired angle, mark an exact guideline on the board and use a miter-gauge extension—a straight piece of wood that screws or bolts to the gauge—to hold the board steady while the cut is made. For cutting wide boards and panels, table extensions and a helper are generally necessary.

The band saw has special problems of control. Because you need to guide the board freehand for curved cuts, be sure to mark guidelines that are especially accurate. And because the throat of the saw can obstruct the movement of the board in the course of a long curve, you must plan your starting point and your movements with care—for certain cuts, the best strategy is to lay out the cutting lines on both faces of the board and flip the board in mid-cut.

With both saws, take the general safety precautions that apply to all power tools—and for a table saw add a few special ones. Stand to the side of the blade—if it binds, the board may shoot backward. Use a push stick to feed the board for a narrow rip cut *(page 27, bottom, center),* and insert a wedge in the kerf of any rip cut that is more than 3 feet long, to prevent the blade from binding *(page 23, top).*

Other shop tools such as the edge-straightening jointer come in handy for occasional jobs. And one homemade tool—a sturdy sawhorse *(pages 54-55)*—is almost a necessity.

Making Straight Cuts with a Table Saw

Ripping a board. Turn the saw on, press the board lightly against the fence with your left hand and hook the last two fingers of your right hand over the fence; use the first two fingers and thumb to push the board toward the blade, and remove your left hand at least 6 inches before the end of the cut. If the distance between the rip fence and the board is 6 inches or more, complete the cut with your right hand, bringing the hand back in a high arc above the table; if the distance between fence and board is less than 6 inches, use a stick to push the work past the blade.

Some boards can be allowed to slide off the far end of the table after the cut is made. For boards longer than 2 feet, however, have a helper ease the board off the table; for wide panels, station another helper at the left of the table to keep the panel flush against the fence.

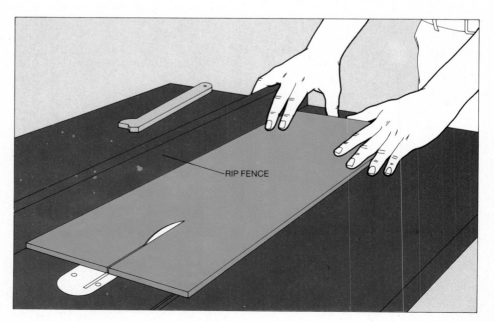

RIP FENCE

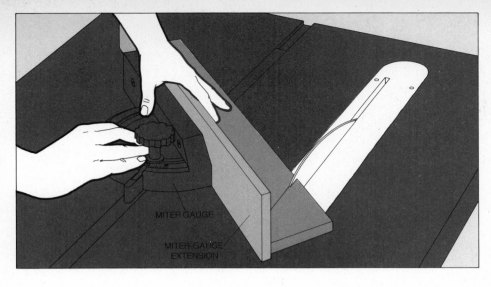

A miter cut. Set the miter gauge, fitted with a smooth wood extension, to the desired angle, then hold the board against the extension with your left hand and, with your right, push the gauge forward. The blade will tend to pull the board off course during the cut; take special care to keep the cutting line on the board aligned with the blade by using firm forward pressure and holding the board tight against the gauge extension.

MITER GAUGE

MITER-GAUGE EXTENSION

Cutting Curves with a Band Saw

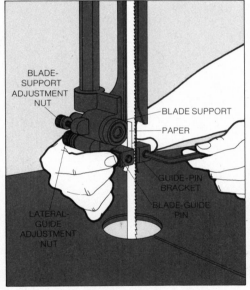

BLADE-SUPPORT ADJUSTMENT NUT

BLADE SUPPORT

PAPER

GUIDE-PIN BRACKET

BLADE-GUIDE PIN

LATERAL-GUIDE ADJUSTMENT NUT

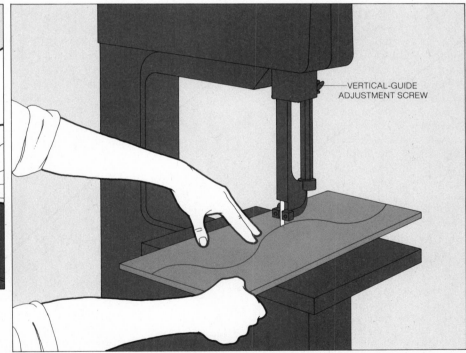

VERTICAL-GUIDE ADJUSTMENT SCREW

1 **Adjusting the blade support and guides.** After putting a new blade in place, turn the blade-support adjustment nut to set a ¹⁄₆₄-inch gap between the support and the back of the blade. Use the lateral guide-adjustment nut to set the edges of the guide-pin brackets flush with the gullets between the teeth of the blade. To adjust the clearance between the guide pins and the blade, loosen the brackets with a hex wrench, wrap a piece of heavy paper around the blade—brown wrapping paper will do—and press the guide pins together against the paper; then tighten the brackets and remove the paper.

2 **Making the cut.** Set the blade guides to a distance of ¼ inch above the board with the vertical guide-adjustment screw, then turn on the saw; feed the board into the blade with your right hand and turn the board with your left to keep the blade on the guideline. Cut at a steady pace—if you stop or move the board too slowly, the blade will burn the wood. At all times, keep both hands well away from the blade; hook the fingers of your right hand over the near edge of the board and move the left hand back whenever it gets within 3 inches of the blade. As you finish the cut, your hands will necessarily draw close to the blade; take care to keep your fingers clear

of it. Pull your hands back by moving them in wide arcs to each side of the blade; turn off the saw and leave the board on the table until the blade has stopped completely.

When a turn is so sharp that the blade tends to bind, do not increase your feeding pressure. If you have reached a point close to the edge of the board, run the blade out of the board through the waste area and then cut back in from another angle. If you have just begun the cut, turn off the motor, backtrack the blade through the cut, and reposition the board so that you can approach the curve from another direction.

The Necessity: A Solid Sawhorse

Making a sawhorse is a traditional test of a carpenter's skill. Construction foremen often ask a new man to build a sawhorse from scratch—and hire him or not, according to the quality of his work. Unlike most tests of skill, the job produces something useful, for a sawhorse is an essential tool in working with wood, and good ones cannot be purchased ready-made. The ones sold as kits, to be assembled from 2-by-4s and metal brackets, are not as desirable as hand-made ones because their brackets can damage saw blades and they are not sturdy enough.

The homemade sawhorse illustrated here resists tipping, is rigid enough to support almost any load and wide enough to stand on comfortably. Its braced shelf stores tools, a wide top serves as a portable workbench, and strong sidepieces make a low scaffold, complete with built-in steps. For general work, most sawhorses have more or less standard dimensions: a length of 42 inches, to support 4-by-8 sheets of plywood; a height of 24 inches, to hold work just above knee height for easy sawing; and a width at the base of 14½ inches, to fit between studs spaced 16 inches apart.

A standard sawhorse. The 1-by-4 legs of this sawhorse, splayed for stability and braced by plywood endpieces, fit snugly into angled notches in the 2-by-4 top; a 1-by-10 shelf, notched for the legs, fits tightly beneath the endpieces. Raised 1-by-2 side braces keep tools from rolling off the shelf and serve as steps when the sawhorse is used as a scaffold; 1-by-2 cross braces beneath the shelf provide extra support and stability for both the shelf and the legs.

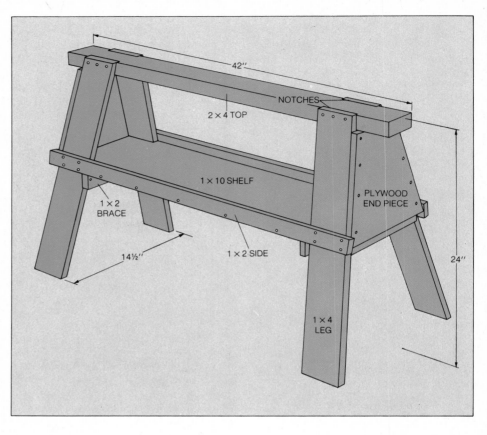

Putting the Pieces Together

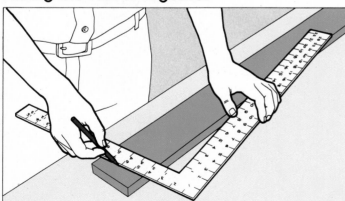

1 **Marking the leg length.** Set the tongue of a framing square across a 1-by-4, align the 4-inch mark on the outside of the tongue and the 24-inch mark at the end of the body with the edge of the board, and draw a line along the tongue to mark the bottom of a leg. At a point 24⅝ inches along the board, use a T bevel (page 28) to mark a parallel line for the top of the leg.

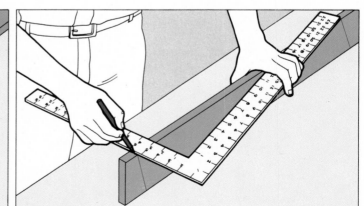

2 **Angling the leg bottom.** Turn the board on its side, align the 5¼-inch mark on the tongue with the bottom line of the leg, align the 24-inch mark on the body with the edge of the board and draw a pencil line along the tongue. Use the T bevel to mark a parallel line at the top of the leg. Cut the leg to length along the lines and use it as a template to cut the other three.

3 **Fitting the legs to the top.** Draw a line across a 42-inch 2-by-4, four inches from one end. Set a T bevel to the 4-in-24 angle of a leg, hold it on the edge of the 2-by-4 at the end of the marked line and slanting out toward the end of the board, and draw a line along its blade. To determine the width of the notch, set a leg against the angled line and draw a line along the other side of the leg; from this line, draw a square line across the 2-by-4 (*inset*) and draw matching lines on the other edge with a T bevel. Mark the other end of the 2-by-4 in the same way.

4 **Marking the depth of the notches.** Set a marking gauge (*page 22, bottom right*) at ⅜ inch and score the top of the 2-by-4 on each side between the square lines (the bottom of the notch will meet the edge of the 2-by-4). Saw along the angled lines and chisel out the waste between saw cuts (*inset*). Lay out and cut the notches at the other end of the 2-by-4, then fasten each leg into a notch with coated eightpenny nails.

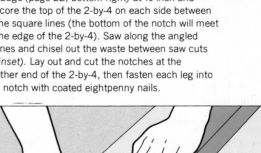

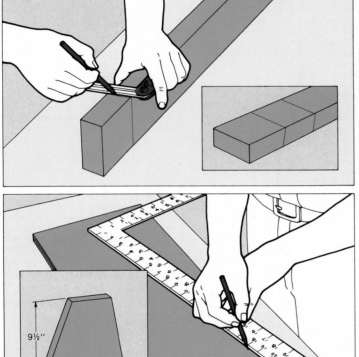

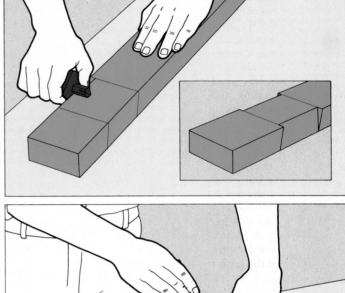

5 **Making the ends.** Set a framing square on a strip of plywood 9½ inches wide, the 24-inch mark on the body against one corner and the 5¼-inch mark on the tongue against the edge, and draw a line from the corner along the body; turn the square over and draw a matching line from the other corner. Draw a square line across the plywood 9½ inches from the end (*inset*), completing a trapezoid shape. Cut the plywood along the trapezoid lines and use it as a template to cut a matching piece. Fasten the endpieces to the legs, positioning them tight beneath the top, with coated eightpenny nails.

6 **Adding a shelf.** In a 1-by-10 board 39½ inches long, lay out notches for the legs by drawing a line ¾ inch from each end. At each corner of the shelf, hold an angled scrap—left over from cutting the legs (*Step 1*)—against the line and the edge of the board, and trace around it. Cut within this outline with a handsaw, try the shelf for fit and pare out the notches with a chisel to fit perfectly. Nail the shelf to the legs and ends.

Cut two 39-inch 1-by-2s to use as sidepieces. Hold each one against the sawhorse, flush with the bottom of the shelf—plane away the edge of the shelf if necessary—and fasten it to the shelf and legs with sixpenny nails. Cut two 1-by-2 braces 10¾ inches long and nail them across the legs, tight beneath the shelf.

The Oldtimer's Techniques of Saw-Sharpening

Using a saw with a dull blade mars the work and damages the tool. The blade cuts slowly and leaves rough edges; the added force needed to push the blade and keep it on course can buckle a handsaw or overheat a power saw until the metal cracks or the teeth break. On a power saw a dull, overheated blade can scorch the wood and ruin the motor.

It makes sense, then, to check your saws for sharpness from time to time. Run your thumb lightly over the tops of the teeth; sharp teeth will prick your skin, but your thumb will slide over dull ones. On a handsaw, visually compare the teeth near the handle—which are rarely used—with the teeth at the middle of the blade: worn teeth will have rounded points; sharp teeth, angled points.

Some blades, particularly those on circular saws, are so inexpensive that they are more easily replaced than resharpened. Others must be left to a profes-

sional: only a professional saw filer's specialized equipment can sharpen a carbide-tipped blade or restore a misshapen circular-saw blade.

But you can resharpen a handsaw or an ordinary circular-saw blade yourself, by simply clamping the blade between long wood strips or in a special saw vise, and touching up the edges of the teeth with a file. For handsaws use a triangular taper file; for circular blades, use either a mill bastard file with a round edge, or a cant (triangular) file with a 120° angle—whichever allows you to sharpen the edges of a saw tooth without touching the adjacent teeth or the valleys between the teeth.

On a handsaw, you can go beyond sharpening to master a craftsman's techniques for completely refitting a badly worn saw (page 58). To begin with, you "joint" the saw—that is, file the tips of the teeth flat, to a uniform height. With

another file you reshape the flattened teeth; then, with a plier-like tool called a saw set, you bend them alternately to the right and to the left. Finally, you sharpen the saw as you would in retouching. Total refitting is an intricate job, in which every step must be performed with special precision. You may have difficulty locating professionals who perform this work properly, but with practice on an inexpensive blade, you can train yourself to meet the high standards of the old-time saw sharpener.

Start any job on a saw blade by checking the teeth for accumulations of pitch and sap, which can clog a file. If necessary, clean the teeth by soaking the blade overnight in kerosene or a solution of either baking soda or lye, then scrubbing it gently with a wire brush. To reduce the need for cleaning, use blades coated with a nonsticking plastic, or oil your steel blades lightly after each use.

Designs for Cutting

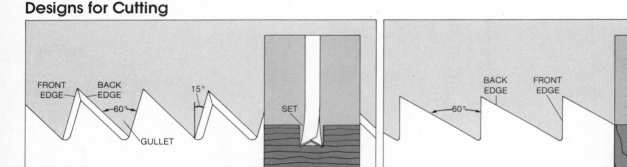

A crosscut handsaw. On each tooth of this saw, two beveled edges meet at a sharp point. The front edge of a tooth is angled 15° from the perpendicular, and meets the back edge of the next tooth at a 60° angle; the valley between two teeth is called a gullet. The teeth are bent, or set, alternately left and right of the blade, and each tooth is beveled on the side opposite the direction of its set.
As you saw, the points of the set teeth score parallel grooves across the wood grain; then, on both the forward and return strokes, the beveled edges of the teeth slice through the wood fibers between the grooves (inset). Because the grooves are farther apart than the thickness of the blade, the saw cuts a kerf that is wider than its blade, and is therefore unlikely to bind.

A ripsaw. The unbeveled edges of each tooth meet at the point in a chisel-like cutting edge. The gullets form 60° angles, like those of a crosscut saw, but the front edge of each tooth is perpendicular to a line along the tops of the teeth.

A ripsaw tooth cuts like a tiny chisel, paring away wood on each forward stroke. The set (inset) may be greater than that of a crosscut saw, cutting wood faster but leaving it rougher.

Two circular blades. On a typical combination blade (left), designed for ordinary crosscuts and rip cuts, the top of each tooth and part of each front edge are filed to form a sharp point; the backs of the teeth are rounded and unfiled. The bevel angles of the filed edges vary from one manufacturer to another, but the bevel of each tooth always slants away from the direction of its set. A blade designed to cut plywood is similar to this blade, but has smaller teeth.

On a hollow-ground planer blade (right), designed for especially smooth cuts, the teeth are arranged in groups of five. Each group consists of one large tooth, called the raker, followed by four smaller teeth, called spurs. The spurs are beveled on both faces and cut wood like the teeth of a crosscut handsaw; the raker, which sits $1/64$ inch below the spurs, is unbeveled and clears the wood chips from the kerf. The teeth of this blade are not set; instead, the area between the hub of the blade and the gullets is ground thinner than the teeth to create a clearance for the body of the blade within the kerf.

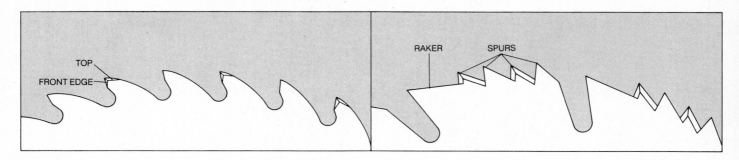

Files for Saws

Points per inch	File
5-5½	7″ regular
6	7″ or 7″ slim
7-8	6″ slim
9-10	5″ or 6″ slim
11-12	4½″ slim or 7″ double extra-slim

Choosing the right file. The left-hand column of this chart lists handsaw sizes according to the number of tooth points per inch of saw blade; the right-hand column lists the corresponding sizes of triangular taper files for sharpening the saws. Manufacturers generally stamp the saw size on the blade near the handle; if you do not find it there, set a ruler just under the saw teeth, with an inch mark directly below a tooth point, and count the number of points in 1 inch, including the two points right above the marks.

Sharpening a Handsaw

Touching up the teeth. Secure the saw, with the handle to your right and the gullets ¼ inch above the wood blocks or vise jaws. At the handle end, place the file in the gullet in front of the first tooth set toward you. On a crosscut saw, like the one shown here, set the file in the gullet at an angle of about 15° from the horizontal, swing it to the left to a 60° angle with the blade, and rotate it about 15° counterclockwise. Push the file forward with a light, even pressure, lift the file from the gullet, and repeat the forward strokes until the beveled edges on each side of the gullet are shiny. Use the same number of strokes to file every second gullet along the blade.

Reverse the saw in the vise and follow the steps above, but swing the handle to the right and rotate it clockwise for each stroke (whatever the saw position, point the file toward the handle).

File a ripsaw with the same method used for a crosscut saw, but keep the file horizontal and perpendicular to the blade, and rotate it 30°

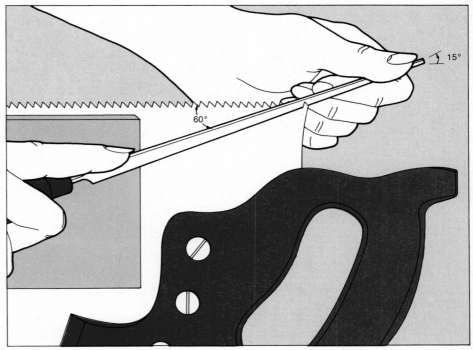

Refitting a Handsaw

1 Jointing the teeth. Secure the saw, with the teeth about 2 inches above the wood blocks or vise jaws holding it. Use a C clamp to fasten a flat file to a small wood block, with half the width of the file extending beyond the edge of the block. Holding the block flat against the saw blades so that the file rests lightly on the tops of the saw teeth, run the file in forward strokes from the heel to the tip of the saw until each tooth has a small flat dot at the point; one or two strokes is usually sufficient.

If you find it hard to keep the block flat against the blade or the file flat on the teeth, use a manufactured hand jointer to secure the file *(inset)*.

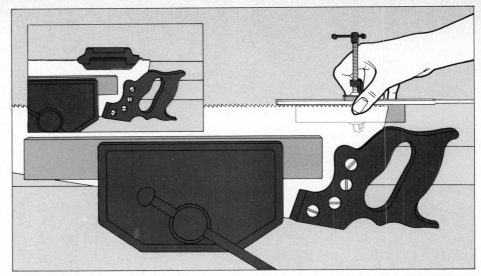

2 Shaping the teeth. Secure the saw as you would for touching up and choose the appropriate triangular file *(page 57, center)*. On ripsaws, and on crosscut saws with teeth that accept a file in the touching-up position, use the procedures for touching up.

On a crosscut saw with teeth so flattened or misshapen that you cannot position the file for touching up, place the file in the front gullet of the first tooth that is set toward you, holding the file horizontal and perpendicular to the saw blade. Rotate the file 15° counterclockwise and file straight across the blade, using pushing strokes only, until the gullet conforms to the shape of the file. Shape every alternate gullet in this way, then reverse the saw and the rotation of the file to shape the other gullets.

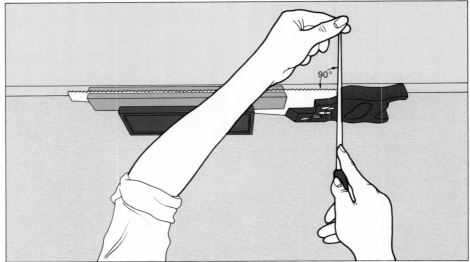

3 Setting the saw. Secure the saw, with the blade about 2 inches above the wood blocks or vise. At the heel of the saw, position the first tooth that is set away from you between the anvil and the plunger of a saw set *(inset)*. This tooth is normally unworn, and does not need resetting; therefore, set the stop-adjusting and anvil-adjusting screws of the saw set so that when you close the handles tightly, the anvil and the plunger pinch the tooth without bending it. (Do not rely on adjusting-screw markings for different saw sizes; make your judgment by eye and feel.) Apply the saw set to every alternate tooth along the saw, squeezing the handles each time; reverse the saw to set the other teeth.

Complete the refitting job by touching up the edges of the teeth. This final touching up is necessary after resetting, even if the teeth were touched up as part of Step 2.

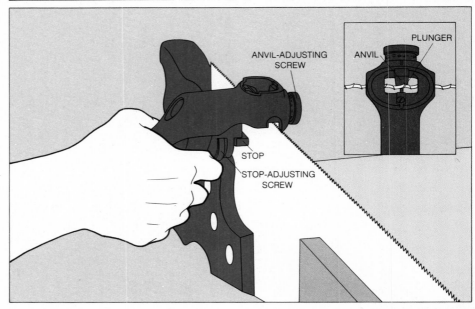

Touching Up a Circular-Saw Blade

1 **Filing the front edges.** Secure the blade—in this example, a combination blade—to the edge of a worktable by driving a nail through a small wood block and the blade center hole into the table edge; the top of the blade should be about 2 inches above the table and the teeth should point clockwise. At the left of the blade, just above the level of the blocks, set the file against the front edge of the first tooth that is set away from you, and swing the handle until the face of the file lies flat against the beveled part of the tooth—you will generally have to move the handle to the left and downward. Keeping the file clear of the bottom of the gullet, file in forward strokes until the bevel is shiny, but do not use more than eight strokes. Use the same number of strokes to file the front edge of each tooth that is set away from you in the part of the blade above the table.

On hollow-ground blades, sharpen the front edge of the teeth on which the bevels face you.

2 **Filing the back edges.** Return to the first tooth you worked on and align the file with the other cutting edge, generally located on the top or back of the tooth in a combination blade, on the back in a planer blade; file this edge as in Step 1 above, to form a sharp point on the tooth. On the rakers of a planer blade, file the point 1/64 inch below the points of the other teeth.

Repeat the procedure on all the teeth set away from you or beveled toward you in the protruding blade section, and rotate the blade clockwise in the vise to get at additional teeth; when you have sharpened every alternate tooth, flip the blade in the vise and sharpen the others.

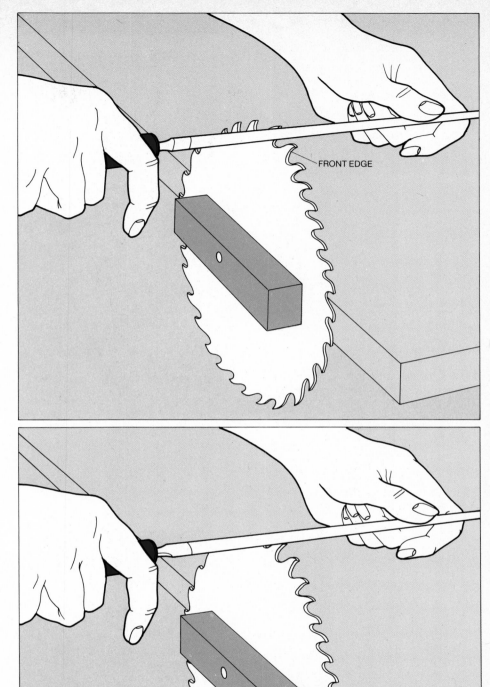

FRONT EDGE

2

Making a Multitude of Holes

A battery of borers. The first three of these seven drill bits, reading counterclockwise from upper left, are designed to leave a smooth surface in wood: the multispur bit cuts plywood without tearing, the Forstner bit cuts a finished hole with a flat recessed bottom, and the star-shaped countersink widens the top of a pilot hole. The next two bits make rough holes: the auger bit in cramped spaces, the expansive bit for large holes. For an electric drill, the preferred bits are the spade bit for most holes, and the hole saw.

The American house is riddled with holes. On the average, more than 600 holes are cut through studs, joists and floors as passageways for pipes and cables; larger holes accept the ducts of a modern heating system; innumerable pilot holes accommodate the screws that fasten every manner of object to wooden surfaces; and wide, shallow holes accept metal hardware.

The tools that carpenters use to make holes today are remarkably like those employed for the last several thousand years. Still essential is the auger bit *(left),* invented by the Romans, held in a brace with the adjustable chuck that was perfected more than a century ago by the British. For shallow holes, the tool most often chosen is the chisel, which traces its ancestry back to the Stone Age. Even newly designed bits and cutters resemble their ancient predecessors and are based on the same fundamental principles.

What has changed, and changed radically, is the power that drives the bits and cutters: it is now less often muscle power than electricity. Although hand tools continue to be popular—and, for some jobs, necessary—most holes that are drilled today are made with the aid of an electric motor.

The electric drill—heavy, powerful and so fast that many models spin their bits at more than 20 revolutions per second—has taken the tedium out of most drilling and reduced the physical requirements for the job. Unfortunately, it has done so at the expense of accuracy and control. A stationary drill press *(page 66)* is a precise tool, but for the portable drills generally used in house carpentry, only drilling jigs can guide a bit to a predetermined depth or hold it firmly in position on a board. Some specialized jigs, like the ones used by locksmiths to make holes in doors, cost hundreds of dollars; most, like the ones shown on pages 65 and 66, are inexpensive and designed for use by home craftsmen; many jigs are homemade. And improvements in the drill itself—a lighter casing, a variable-speed motor and newly designed handles and switches—have restored some of the control that was lost with the advent of electric motors.

Not all holes are made with drill bits, because not all holes are round. Straight-sided holes are best made by blades rather than bits. Here too, electric power applied to traditional cutters is bringing ease and speed to what had been an arduous job. The large rectangular holes that pass heating and cooling ducts through floors and ceilings are best cut with a power tool—a saber saw or a portable circular saw. And even the shallow rectangular holes, called mortises, that hold door hinges and lock plates, can be cut not only in the old way, with a mallet and chisel, but also with one of the newest power tools of all—the router.

How to Bore Holes Straight, Clean and True

In principle, drilling holes is the simplest operation in carpentry; in practice, it can be one of the most frustrating. No matter how careful your planning and how steady your hand, drilling jobs never quite match the textbook rules: the drill will not fit into the cramped space between joists, it veers sideways in a bolt-hole that must be perfectly straight, or it whips around and splinters wood as it breaks through a board.

You may be able to avoid these difficulties if you use the right tools and a repertoire of time-tested carpenter's tricks. Filing flat spots on the round shank of a bit will help it stay put in a power-drill chuck, for example, and a homemade guide like the one on page 66 helps prevent skittering when you drill at a shallow angle.

The basic tool for virtually any drilling task—from making a tiny pilot hole for a wood screw to boring a 2½-inch opening for a plumbing pipe—is the portable electric drill; the type preferred by most amateurs is the ⅜-inch model that has a variable-speed trigger switch and a reversing switch.

The drill should be equipped with a double-insulating plastic case, which will prevent electrical shock if the bit runs into live electrical wires, and a lock on the reversing switch to prevent you from changing directions while the motor is running. A well-designed drill has its handle at the back of the case and an auxiliary handle to help you counter the twisting torque from a large bit.

On small jobs, particularly in hard-to-reach places, you may want to drill holes with hand tools. For pilot holes less than ¹¹/₆₄ inch wide, a particular favorite with carpenters is the push drill (often called a Yankee, a trademark of the company that makes it)—a spring-loaded rod about a foot long, with a set of bits stored in its handle. An old-fashioned "egg-beater" drill can make holes up to ¼ inch wide; it is easier to control than a power drill, but takes more time and effort. For larger holes in cramped quarters, such as the spaces between studs or joists, a brace and an auger bit can be handy if the brace has a ratchet mechanism that allows it to turn in tight quarters.

Although a drill press—a large power drill permanently mounted on a stationary stand—seldom is found on commercial construction jobs, it is a workshop tool that can be very helpful in home carpentry. Work must be brought to it, and it cannot handle large panels (the standard 15-inch home drill press can drill to the center of a board 15 inches wide). However, it is faster, more precise and more versatile than other drills, and perfect for repetitious tasks, such as drilling a set of holes for dowels or louvers.

Almost all of these drills have a three-jawed chuck, which will accept a bit with a cylindrical or hexagonal shank. The only exception is the chuck of a brace, which has a pair of jaws, each with a V-shaped notch in the center; it is designed for the four-sided shank of many auger bits (opposite corners of the bit fit into the notched jaws), but it also will accept a hexagonal shank.

The biggest problem that arises in the course of a drilling job is controlling the bit after it enters the wood. To set the bit for a precise hole, you may need an inexpensive drill guide or a self-centering jig (page 65); to control the depth of the hole, you can wrap tape around the bit at the correct depth or use a factory-made metal jig that clamps to the bit. Even with these aids, you occasionally will drill a hole in the wrong place or at the wrong angle. To correct such a mistake, glue a tightly fitting dowel or wooden matchstick into the hole, wait for the glue to set, and redrill the hole from scratch.

Choosing the Right Bit

Bits for holes up to ½ inch. A twist bit *(top)*—often called a twist drill or simply a drill—is generally manufactured as an all-purpose tool that will drill through plastic and metal as well as wood. Less common is a bit, made especially for wood, that looks exactly like it but has a sharper tip—82° instead of the standard 118°. A brad-point bit *(bottom)*—available in ¹/₁₆-inch intervals from ¼ to ½ inch—is a special bit that is preferred for dowel holes and exposed woodwork because it cuts a very smooth hole. The point at the center of the shaft guides the bit while sharp lips at the outside actually cut the hole.

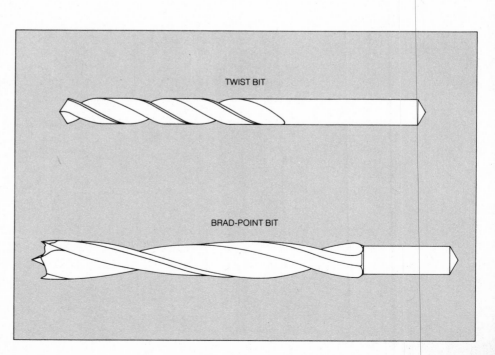

TWIST BIT

BRAD-POINT BIT

Bits for holes up to 1 inch wide. A spade bit *(top)*, the most versatile and inexpensive of the larger bits, is used with a power drill to cut holes quickly; it tends to wander in deep holes and to leave ragged edges.

The more expensive single-twist auger bit *(center)* can be used in a hand brace or a power drill; it is slower but easier to control and leaves a cleaner, more precise hole. As this bit is pulled into the wood by a feed screw at the tip, spurs at the outside score the hole edges and horizontal cutters scrape away wood chips.

An electrician's bit *(bottom)* works on the same principle but is used for deeper holes and rougher work, particularly in the framing of a house; it is more flexible because it has no solid central shaft, and more durable because it has no cutting spur that can be ruined by nails.

Two special-purpose bits. A Forstner bit has a flat, disc-shaped head that contains sharp cutting edges. It is expensive and slow, but has certain advantages: it can drill into any sort of grain, including end grain, it can drill at an angle to the board face without sliding off because its sharpened outer edges dig into the wood, and it makes an almost perfectly flat-bottomed hole —an advantage when you need a large counterbore or are drilling partway through a board.

A multispur bit, used mainly in drill presses, has a sharply pointed tip surrounded by a ring of teeth. It is particularly useful on thin paneling and veneered plywood because it cuts cleanly without shredding the surface.

Countersink bits to recess wood screws. The most common countersink, designed for use with a power drill, is the combination tool *(near right)* that in one step drills a pilot hole, bevels the top of the hole for a screwhead and, if required, counterbores a hole for a wooden plug. Available for screws from No. 6 to No. 12, this tool is essentially a hollow tube, slipped over the shank of a twist bit and fastened with a setscrew; the depth of the pilot hole is determined by the position of the countersink on the shank.

If a pilot hole already has been drilled, if a screwhead is too large for a combination countersink or if you need to countersink only a few holes, use an ordinary countersink. The traditional type *(center)* must be used in a hand brace; a newer style *(far right)* is designed for power drills.

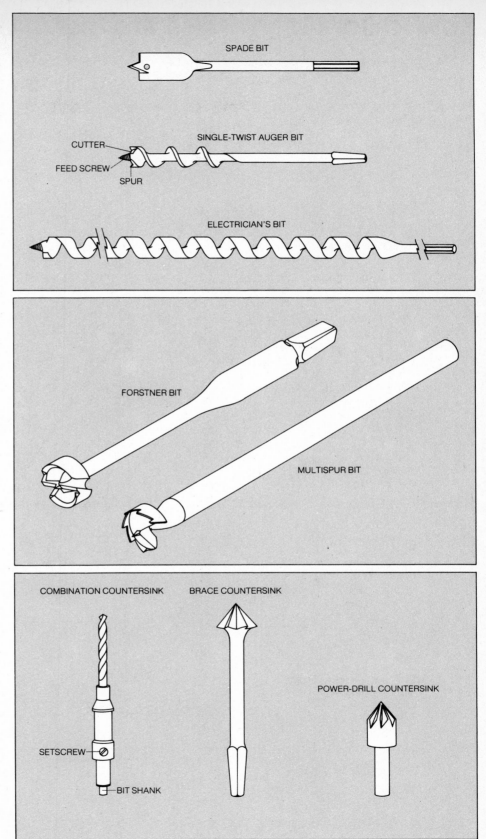

SPADE BIT

SINGLE-TWIST AUGER BIT

CUTTER
FEED SCREW
SPUR

ELECTRICIAN'S BIT

FORSTNER BIT

MULTISPUR BIT

COMBINATION COUNTERSINK   BRACE COUNTERSINK

POWER-DRILL COUNTERSINK

SETSCREW

BIT SHANK

Two Ways to Hold a Power Drill

Cradling for a small bit. To start a twist or a brad-point bit, push an awl into the wood at the center mark for the hole. Grip the drill handle with one hand, cradle the underside of the drill with the other and set the point of the bit in the awl hole. Gently press the drill into the wood and squeeze the trigger slowly until the bit starts to turn. When the bit has made a hole that is approximately ⅛ inch deep, increase the speed of the drill to its maximum and bear down firmly. When the bit has drilled almost to the full depth of the board, reduce the pressure but maintain the speed of the drill as the bit bores through the last fraction of an inch. If the hole must be perfectly perpendicular to the surface of the wood, set a combination square against the board and sight the bit against it (inset) or use one of the jigs depicted opposite.

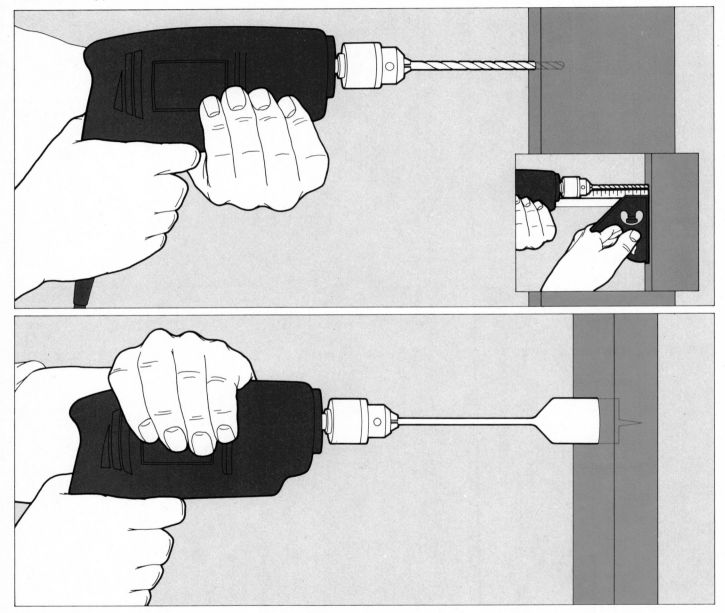

Steadying a large bit. To drive a bit with large cutting edges, such as a spade or Forstner bit, hold the drill handle with one hand and grasp the top of the drill firmly with the other, a grip that resists the twisting tendency of the drill better than the cradling grip illustrated at the top of this page. Press the bit firmly into the awl hole and begin the hole at a fairly high speed.

If the bit binds momentarily, maintain speed but pull the drill back a fraction of an inch, then bear down again (slowing the speed will increase the tendency to bind). When the bit nears the other side of the board, reduce pressure and brace yourself; the drill may jerk and bind as it breaks through. Turn off the drill as soon as the bit is cleanly through the board.

With an auger bit, work at a somewhat slower speed. If the motor begins to labor, press the trigger to maintain speed. Reduce the drilling speed as you come close to the end of the hole; when the feed screw breaks through the other side, the bit no longer will pull itself into the wood and you must bear down on the bit with additional force to finish boring the hole.

The Use of Hand Drills

Using an egg-beater drill. For a few small holes, many carpenters prefer this old-fashioned manual drill. Set the bit point in an awl hole, press the drill lightly against the wood and turn the crank clockwise. When the bit breaks through the board, continue to crank clockwise as you pull the bit out—cranking counterclockwise will release the bit from the chuck.

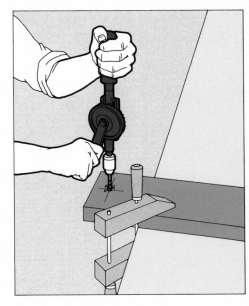

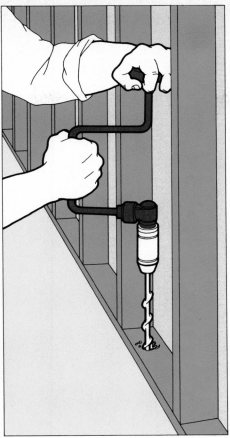

A ratchet brace for cramped quarters. Where there is too little space to align a power drill properly, use a brace, adjusting the ratchet setting of the brace for a clockwise sweep. Set the feed screw of the auger bit into the awl hole, press hard on the brace head with one hand and slowly swing the handle in half circles with the other until the feed screw is buried in the wood and the bit begins to bore. If the feed screw does not dig into the wood, make sure you are holding the brace steady; side-to-side movement loosens the screw. When the bit breaks through the board, reverse the ratchet adjustment and pull the handle to back the bit out.

Guides and Jigs for Precision Work

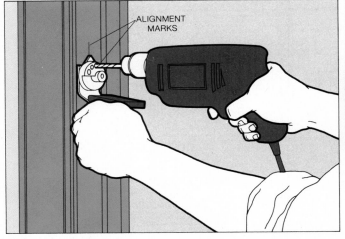

A hand-held drill guide. A revolving selector in this guide has holes of the common sizes of small bits to position a bit for perfect right-angle drilling. Marks on the guide can be aligned with marks on the wood to help locate the hole.

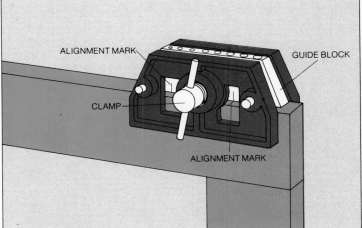

A self-centering doweling jig. The guide block of this jig has holes for five common dowel sizes and is automatically centered by a clamp; it sets dowel holes perfectly centered in board edges—as for corner joints on a door. To align the jig, mark a square line across the board edge for each hole, line up the matching guide-block mark, and tighten the clamp. Drill the hole with a twist or a brad-point bit.

A homemade angle jig. Cut perfectly square ends on a scrap of 4-by-4 about 1 foot long and, about 1 inch from one end, drill a hole of the desired diameter at a perfect right angle to the face of the board. Set a T bevel to the desired angle of the hole you are planning to drill and hold the handle of the bevel against the end of the board, so that the cutting edge crosses the path of the bored straight hole; mark a line along the blade, and an X inside the angle of the T bevel. Using a miter box, cut the 4-by-4 along the marked line (*page* 30, *Step 1*).

Temporarily nail the jig to the board you plan to drill, with its sawed face down (*inset*), and use the hole as a guide for the drill bit.

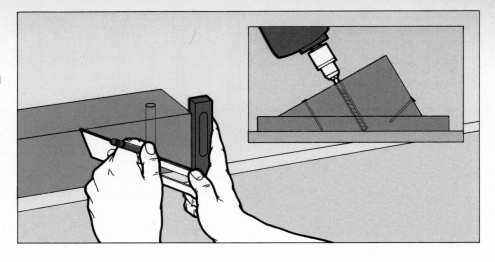

For Perfect Holes, a Drill Press

1 **Adjusting the table.** With the bit in the drill chuck, fasten the board to the drill-press table with C clamps. Hold the table and loosen the locking handle that fastens the table to the column, then raise or lower the table by simultaneously lifting it and swinging it from side to side. When the tip of the drill bit is about ¼ inch above the board, tighten the locking handle and move the safety collar on the column to a position just beneath the table. Adjust the stop nut and the lock nut on the calibrated stop rod to set the depth of the planned hole.

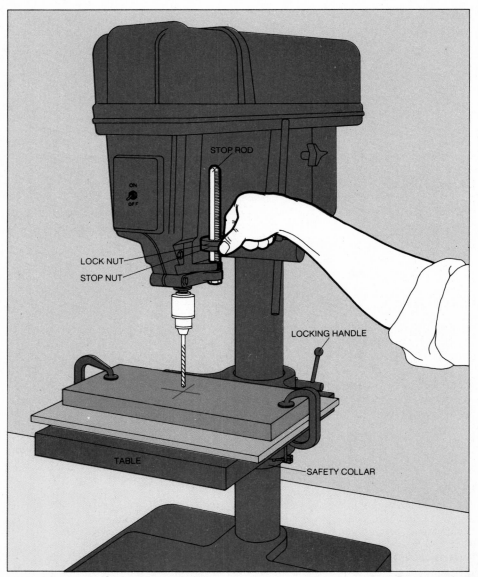

2 Drilling the hole. With the drill off, loosen the clamps that hold the board and turn the feed lever until the bit almost touches the wood; then shift the board to clamp it with the center of the planned hole directly beneath the tip of the bit. Let the bit rise to the stop, turn the motor on and slowly lower the bit into the wood, using light pressure on the feed lever.

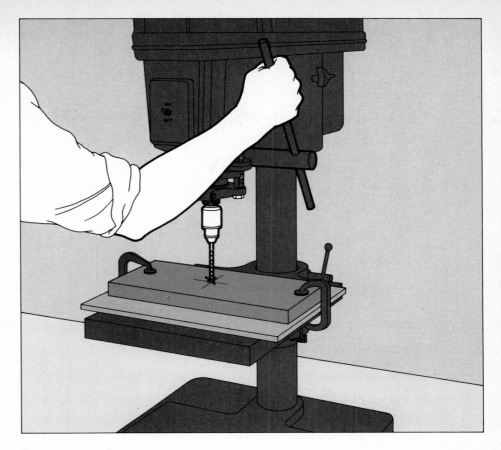

Drill-Press Setups for Angled Holes

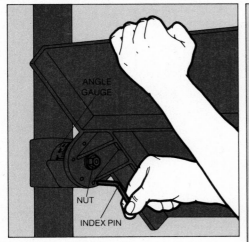

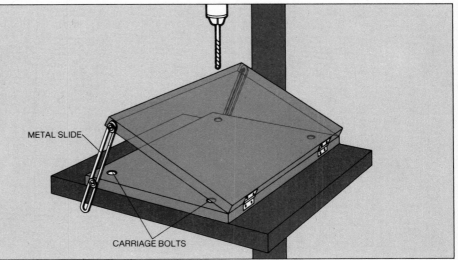

A factory-made tilting table. If your drill-press table pivots on the clamp that fastens it to the column, as in the model shown here, loosen the nut at the base of the table; remove the index pin from its hole in the base and tilt the table to the desired angle. To drill a hole at an angle of 45°, 90°, 135° or 180°, slide the index pin through the hole for the angle and tighten the nut; for other angles, set the index pin aside, align the arrow on the tabletop with the correct reading on the angle gauge and tighten the nut.

A homemade tilting table. If your machine does not have a tilting table, cut two pieces of 1-by-12 to 9½ by 11 inches; hinge them together lengthwise. Set the assembly on the drill-press table with the hinges at one side; on the lower board, mark the location of the table's mounting holes. Drill and counterbore a hole at each mark and fasten the board to the table with ¼-inch carriage bolts and wing nuts.

Fasten 8½-inch metal desk-lid slides to the opposite sides of the boards with wood screws and washers. To use the table, temporarily bolt the lower board to the drill-press table, raise the upper board to the angle you want, checking with a T bevel, then lock the upper board by tightening the wood screws of the slides. Fasten the work to the angled table with C clamps and drill it in the usual way.

Four Ways to Make Large Holes

Although the spade and auger bits shown on pages 62-65 can bore holes as wide as 1½ inches, most holes more than 1 inch wide are made with a different set of tools. For holes between 1 and 3 inches in diameter, needed mainly for plumbing drains and vents, special bits are used; openings still larger than that—circular for stovepipes and round ducts, rectangular for chimneys, electrical outlets and square ducts—are cut with saws.

The drilled holes ordinarily require an electric drill—either the standard ⅜-inch size or, for particularly wide, deep holes, a ½-inch drill, available at rental agencies. The preferred bits are hole saws—hollow metal cylinders with sawlike teeth, which fit onto a separate shaft called a mandrel *(right)*. Hole saws can be fitted with such accessories as bit extensions—some as long as 4 feet—for very deep or inaccessible holes. If you must drill an odd-sized hole or lack the right hole saw for a standard one, you can substitute a brace and an expansive bit *(bottom)*, which has a cutter adjustable to a range of diameters.

For sawing holes, the keyhole saw on page 46 will serve, but a faster, more common tool is a saber saw, used freehand or with a yokelike guide that guarantees perfect circles. A saber saw also can be used for large rectangular holes, but professional carpenters prefer a portable circular saw; to start each side of the cut, they "plunge" the blade of the saw into the middle of a panel, making what is called a pocket cut, then finish the side of the opening by using the saw in the normal way.

Bits for Holes Up to 3 Inches Wide

A hole saw. Slide the mandrel through the center of the hole saw *(inset)* and secure it with the mandrel nut (on some large saws, the mandrel screws into the hole saw), then clamp the shank of the mandrel in the chuck of the drill. Mark the center of the hole with an awl and start the hole with the twist bit at the end of the mandrel; when the saw begins to cut, grasp the drill firmly to resist its twist. When the twist bit breaks through the wood, withdraw the saw and finish the job from the other side.

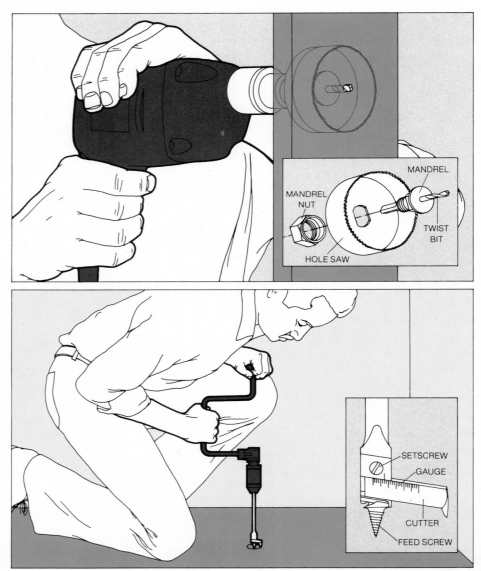

An expansive bit. Loosen the setscrew at the head of the bit *(inset)* and slide the cutter along its groove to the diameter of the desired hole, as indicated on the cutter gauge, then tighten the setscrew; if precision is essential to the job, check the cutter setting by drilling a trial hole.

Use the bit as you would an auger bit *(page 65, top right)* but take special pains to keep the brace perfectly vertical, so that the cutter shaves away the wood evenly. As the hole deepens, bear down hard on the brace; otherwise the feed screw will strip out of the wood and stop pulling.

Saws for Openings Any Size You Need

A saber-saw guide for a perfect circle. One end of the guide at right is fastened to the center of a planned hole, and the other is fastened to a saber saw. To set up the guide, drill a ¼-inch hole at a point on the edge of the planned hole and insert the saber-saw blade in this starter hole. Slide the guide through the slots in the saw shoe, drive a nail through one of the holes at the end of the guide into the exact center of the planned hole and clamp the guide to the saw shoe. Start the saw and cut the hole by pivoting the guide around the nail.

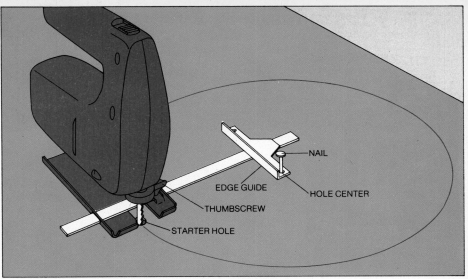

NAIL

EDGE GUIDE

HOLE CENTER

THUMBSCREW

STARTER HOLE

A rectangular hole with a saber saw. For a hole less than 8 inches on a side, mark the outline of the hole with a pencil and combination square and drill a ¼-inch hole at each corner. Insert the saw blade in one hole and cut along the outline; at each corner, turn the saw off and turn it to cut the adjacent side of the rectangle.

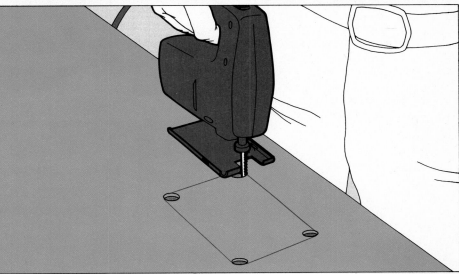

A rectangular hole with a circular saw. To cut a hole more than 8 inches to a side, set the blade of the saw ¼ inch deeper than the thickness of the wood. Rest the toe of the saw on the wood, holding the heel and blade above the wood. Retract the blade guard with your free hand and align the blade directly above one side of the hole; then start the saw, slowly lower the blade into the wood until the base plate rests flat on the wood and cut to the corner of the hole.

Caution: This is the most dangerous part of the job; hold the saw with special firmness and be prepared to turn it off immediately if it goes out of control. Remove the saw and cut the other sides of the hole in the same way. Where precision is important, stop your cuts short of the corners and finish them with a keyhole saw.

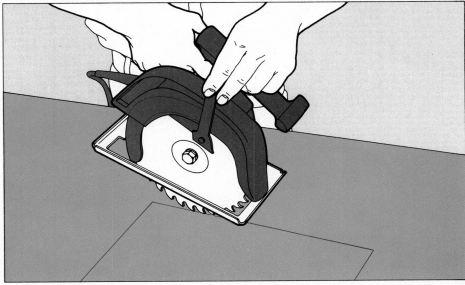

The Rectangular Holes Called Mortises

There are several kinds of the rectangular holes called mortises, and the kind you have to make determines the tools and techniques you should use. Some mortises are precise but shallow, like the recess that houses a hinge. Others are rough and deep, like the pocket for the end of a hand-hewn beam. Still others are both precise and deep, like mortises in door and window joints.

The most common tool for both deep and shallow mortises is a chisel. However, shallow mortises are cut quickly and accurately by a router (the router gives round corners, but you can buy round-cornered hinges and other hardware to fit router-cut mortises). Deep mortises are made with a drill and a chisel, a mallet and a special mortise chisel, or a mortiser—an attachment for a drill press that performs the seemingly impossible feat of drilling a square hole.

The best all-around chisel, called a heavy-duty butt chisel, has a metal cap at the end of a solid plastic handle and can safely be pounded with a hammer. One face of the blade is flat; the other is beveled along the sides as well as on the cutting edge. This sturdy tool is sometimes called "everlasting" by carpenters, because it is virtually indestructible in normal use and can be sharpened again and again *(pages 102, 104-105)*.

For deep precision mortising, however, as in the joints of window sashes or panel doors *(page 132)*, the quickest and simplest tool is the special mortise chisel, which must be used with a large, rectangular wooden mallet. Together they cut and pry out wood in a single step, generally for a mortise exactly as wide as the chisel blade. Long, thick and heavy, the mortise chisel can take hard mallet blows without twisting as it enters the wood, and the mortise it makes is so smooth that it rarely needs paring.

More expensive but most precise of all for accurate deep mortises is the mortiser attachment on a drill press. Fortunately, one size will do many jobs—depth is adjustable, and it is possible, by boring square adjoining holes, to build mortises of any width or length. The attachment is easy to use, even without much practice, and it is fast, speeding the tedious job of making many mortises in a single spell of work. However, the time required to set up the attachment makes it slower to use than a mortise chisel when only a few mortises are needed.

Chiseling a Shallow Mortise

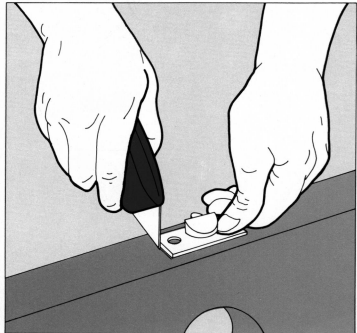

1 Marking the mortise. Press the hardware—in this example, the faceplate of a door catch—against the wood and score along its edges with a utility knife, using repeated light strokes to cut the wood fiber so that the chisel will be less likely to splinter the surface.

If the mortise will be open on one side, as for a door hinge, mark the mortise depth on the open side with a marking gauge *(page 22)*.

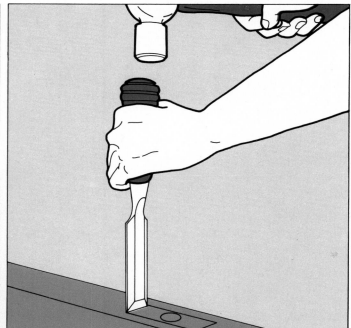

2 Cutting the edges. Set a heavy-duty butt chisel to the wood, with its bevel facing into the outlined area and its cutting edge on the score line. Holding the blade vertical, tap the chisel with a hammer. Cut slightly deeper than the thickness of the hardware—you can gauge the depth of the cut directly on the chisel blade by holding a thumbnail at the junction of the blade and the wood, then pulling the chisel out of the cut. Repeat the cuts along all the score lines.

3 **Scoring.** Set the blade vertically across the outlined area, about ¼ inch from one end, with the bevel facing outward, then slant the chisel slightly toward the bevel side and away from your hammer hand. Tap the chisel to a depth slightly less than the thickness of the hardware. Repeat this cut at ⅜-inch intervals to within ⅜ inch of the far end of the mortise (*left*). Reverse the chisel and remove the ⅜-inch chips, holding the chisel so that the bevel is almost horizontal and is at the full depth of the mortise (*right*).

Finally, reverse the chisel a second time to clear out the far end of the mortise.

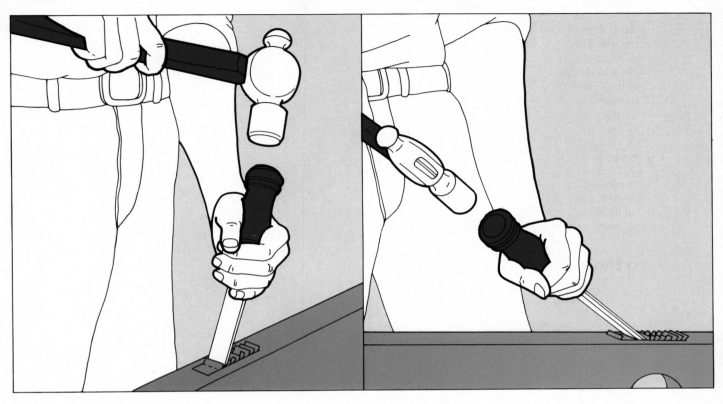

Finishing the Mortise

Paring a closed mortise. Hold the chisel, bevel down, with the heel of one hand against the end of the handle and the thumb of the other on the flat side of the blade. Make light shaving strokes parallel to the grain along the bottom of the mortise so that you produce a smooth, even surface. Test-fit the hardware occasionally to check the depth of the mortise.

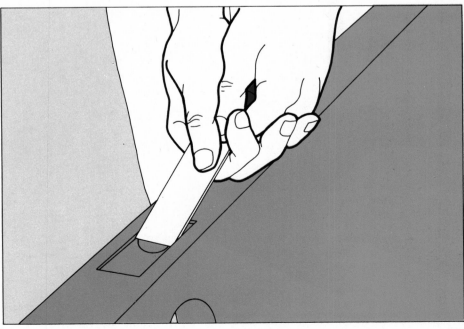

Paring an open mortise. Position the chisel, bevel up, at the open side of the mortise, setting the flat side of the blade even with the mortise bottom. Grip the chisel as you would for a closed mortise, holding the index finger of your forward hand as far back from the cutting edge as the width of the mortise, so that on each stroke, you can stop the blade when the edge reaches the far side. Make light shaving strokes, working at about an 80° angle to the grain.

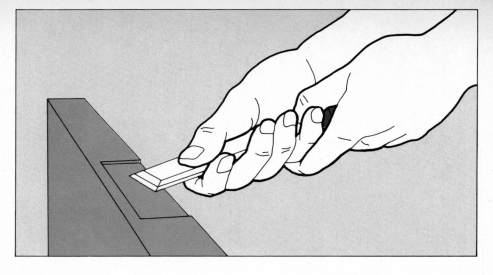

Routing a Shallow Mortise

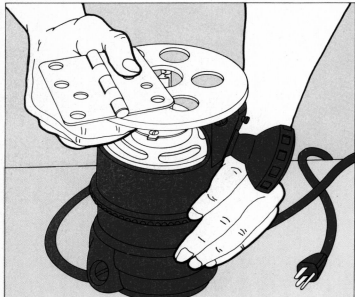

1 Setting the bit. Fit a straight bit in a router, hold the router with its bottom up, and set the hardware alongside the bit as a guide for adjusting the cutting depth.

Score the outline and cut the edges of the mortise (*page 70, Steps 1 and 2*). If you plan to leave the corners round for round-cornered hardware, use especially light strokes at the corners—if the knife point is pressed too hard, it will tend to follow a straight path between fibers and stray from the rounded outlines.

2 Routing out the wood. For a closed mortise, set the router bit over the board at the center of the mortise outline, with the router slightly tilted; turn on the motor and lower the bit into the wood. For an open mortise, start the cut at the edge of the board, as on page 97, middle. With the base plate flat on the wood, guide the bit to remove the wood within the outlined area. As you work, try to keep the outline marks between the bit and your line of vision, but do not lean completely over the router. For a closed mortise, you may have to interrupt your work and move over to the opposite side of the board to finish the job.

If you need to have square corners in your mortise, use a chisel to square off the rounded corners that are left by the router.

A Mortise in Rough Lumber

1 Starting with a drill. Choose a drill bit as close in size to the mortise width as you can, mark the bit shank with tape for the mortise depth, and drill repeatedly inside the mortise outline. Locate the holes to barely touch one another and to come within 1/16 inch of the outline of the mortise.

2 Finishing with a chisel. Remove most of the remaining wood with a heavy-duty butt chisel and a hammer, holding the chisel vertical with the bevel facing out of the mortise. Then hold the chisel in two hands with the bevel facing into the mortise and pare the sides roughly vertical.

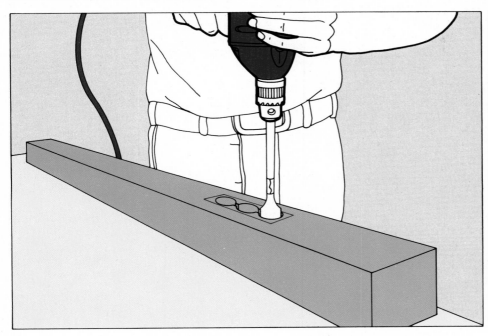

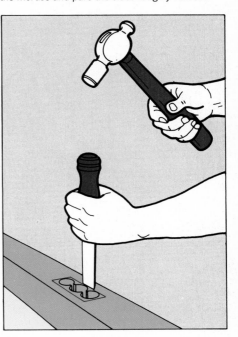

Cutting Deep Holes with a Mortise Chisel

1 Marking the mortise. To fit the mortise precisely to the width of the chisel blade, mark it with precision tools: outline the sides with a mortising gauge (*page 133*), and the ends with a combination square and a utility knife; then use the knife and square to score a series of lines across the outline. Score the first line across the center of the outline and score lines 1/8 inch to each side; then, working toward the ends of the mortise, score lines at 3/8-inch intervals, with the last lines about 1/8 inch from the ends.

Use tape to mark the depth of the mortise on the back and front of the mortise-chisel blade.

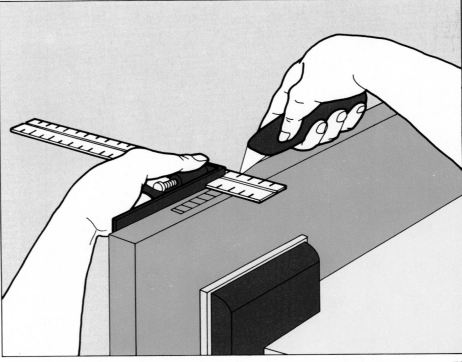

2 Aligning the chisel. Use a chisel that is exactly as wide as the mortise. Standing at one end of the mortise outline, hold the handle with one hand and use the other to set the blade, bevel facing away, in the center score line.

Check to be sure that the sides of the chisel align with the sides of the outline.

3 Cutting. Hold the chisel blade exactly vertical and strike the end of the handle hard, using a wooden mallet with a large rectangular head, until the bevel is driven into the wood. Remove the chisel, turn the bevel to face you, and align the cutting edge with the first score line on your side of the center line. Drive the entire bevel into the wood, then pull the handle down and to-ward you to pry out a chip. Turn the chisel again, align it with the first score line on the far side of the center line, and repeat the procedure. Continue making cuts until you reach the full depth of the mortise and have cut to within ⅛ inch of the outline ends. To finish the mortise, turn the bevel to face inside the mortise and tap lightly with the mallet until the ends are vertical.

Drilling Square Holes with a Drill-Press Mortiser

A mortising attachment. In the assembly at right, a yoke clamped to the neck of a drill press holds a square, hollow chisel below the chuck of the press. The chuck itself holds a specialized drill bit that turns within the chisel. While the tip of the bit cuts a round hole, the chisel chops corners on each side, and the auger-like shaft of the bit forces wood chips up and out through a slot in the front of the chisel. The depth adjustment of the drill press sets the depth of the mortise; long or wide mortises are made by drilling square holes side by side.

CHUCK —

— YOKE

— CHISEL

— BIT

How the Housewright Hand-Hews Beams

On the American frontier, a woodworker began at the source of his material—the tree. He made his own lumber from scratch with two axes: a poleax to fell the tree and make rough kerfs in the log, and a broadax to slice away wood between kerfs and square the sides. The poleax has a straight handle and a head weighing about 4½ pounds, while the broadax has a curved handle (to keep knuckles from being skinned on wood) and a heavier head.

The lumber-making process began with selection of the tree; the housewright judged the size of the log from the smaller end of the trunk. Pine and oak were the woods most often used for log homes; weather-resistant walnut or locust were sometimes used for sill logs. The best trees were saved for floor joists and shingles, which have to be straight.

After felling his log, the housewright cut a rounded depression called a saddle notch at the larger end of the log, then rolled the log over and raised it on two smaller logs called saddle blocks. The notch on the underside kept the log steady during the shaping process, and placing the log off the ground ensured that the ax would not strike the ground and ruin its edge (resharpening might take half a day).

The housewright next marked the sides of the log for hewing, using the equivalent of today's chalk line—a string dipped in a tin cup of berry juice, preferably from the deep-purple pokeberry. His skill and sense of balance then were revealed as he mounted the log, spread his feet apart, swung his poleax above his head and brought the ax down into the side of the log to score a kerf. He swung his ax repeatedly, sidestepping his way down the log and scoring kerfs in a smooth, fluid motion.

To hew the kerfed beam square and smooth, the housewright next placed one knee on the log and worked his way down its length, shaving off sections with his broadax. The bark—which was left on the top and bottom of the log—helped to hold the ax head against the wood and kept it from ricocheting dangerously.

The knack of using these tools to convert a tree into a neatly hand-hewn beam is all but lost. It is kept alive by a few modern housewrights, such as Douglas Reed of Sharpsburg, Maryland, who has helped restore a number of historic log buildings in that area. "Today we have some awkward notion that hand-hewn beams should look as if a madman butchered them," says Reed. But in the days of the early settlers, he points out, a beam that had been skillfully hewn with an ax came out looking as smooth as if it had been finished with an adz. A seasoned workman sought to leave half the pokeberry mark visible on the log after hewing—and the best did.

Professional Methods for Sharpening Drill Bits

Drilling with a dull bit takes unnecessary time and effort; worse, it can break the bit, cause the drill to slip or ruin a drill motor. Small, inexpensive bits should be discarded and replaced when dull; larger, more costly bits should be sharpened. And though a professional sharpener can do the job for you, you can easily learn to do a professional job yourself.

Part of the job consists in knowing exactly how the bit was shaped to begin with—the lengths and angles of the cutting edges on the tip of the bit. These anatomical details are as important as the sharpness of the bit: a bit with unequal cutting edges will work off-center and cut an oversized hole; a bit with inadequate clearance between its head and shaft will bind and overheat.

Bits with delicate edges and complex anatomies must be sharpened by hand, preferably with files and whetstones especially fitted to the particular bit. An auger-bit file and a whetstone, for example, will hone the cutting edges of an auger bit without damaging the adjacent parts. (Since most brand-new auger bits should get a preliminary sharpening before their first use, these tools are a worthwhile investment.) Triangular stones and files are ideal for sharpening the fluted edges of a countersink bit.

To restore the cutting edges of twist and spade bits—the ones generally used with an electric drill—you will need a grinding wheel with a tool rest and a few simple accessories. A homemade jig (opposite, bottom) sets the correct angles for a twist bit, and a drill gauge—essentially a combination of a protractor and a ruler—checks the angles and lip lengths of the sharpened bit; a stop collar that sets a bit firmly against the tool rest (page 79) enables you to grind the wings of a spade bit symmetrically.

Caution: The innocent-looking grinding wheel is a dangerous tool because its high-speed rotation—generally more than 3500 rpm—generates powerful centrifugal force. It can strike off fast-moving, hot bits of metal and if damaged, it can disintegrate, exploding like a grenade in a shower of lethal fragments. When using one, follow all safety precautions (opposite, right).

If you are buying a new wheel, choose a 5- to 7-inch aluminum oxide wheel with a grit rating of 100 and a vitrified, or glasslike, bond (the bond is the medium used to form the grains of abrasive material into a stable wheel). Before mounting the wheel, check it visually for cracks or chips, then suspend it on a dowel or pencil inserted through the center hole and tap it lightly with a wooden mallet or screwdriver handle. Unless it is a wheel bonded with rubber or organic material, you should hear a clear metallic ring. If it is chipped or cracked or fails to ring clearly, replace it.

After mounting and using the wheel, check it periodically for roundness and wear. A shiny, glazed look indicates that the pores of the wheel are clogged with metal dust and particles. A glazed wheel will overheat and ruin a bit applied to it; you can recondition the wheel with a tool called a starwheel dresser, which hooks on the tool rest and scrapes the wheel face with sharp, star-shaped steel teeth. Do not dress a wheel down more than 1 inch below its original diameter.

Between sharpenings, store your bits in partitioned boxes or in canvas rolls, and clean them regularly to retard the dulling process. Use fine sandpaper or an emery cloth to remove rust and wood sap. To clean the twist of a bit, dip a short length of manila rope in kerosene, then in powdered pumice (available at drugstores), and wrap it around the flutes; to clean the screw point of an auger bit, use a piece of stiff paper, such as an index card.

Cutting Angles of Basic Bits

A twist bit. Two ridges called "lands" spiral around the central shaft, or web, of a twist bit. At the cutting end, the lands are ground to meet at an angle of 118° (82° on some special wood bits), forming two flats, called point surfaces, that converge along a center chisel edge. The front edge of each point surface, called the cutting lip, is slightly higher than the back edge, or heel. The clearance between the two allows the body of the bit to follow easily behind the lips as they cut away wood; the shavings move along the spirals of the lands and out of the hole.

The cutting lips are naturally the first parts of the bit to dull—the edges of the lips become slightly rounded, their clearance above the heels decreases and the bit binds and overheats.

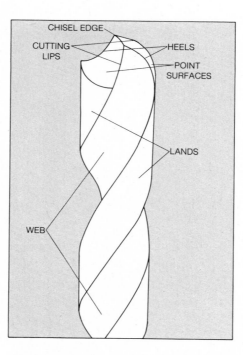

CHISEL EDGE
CUTTING LIPS
HEELS
POINT SURFACES
LANDS
WEB

A spade bit. This flat-bladed bit has a point, or spur, that bites into the wood and steadies the bit on center while winglike cutting lips chisel the hole. The edges of the lips and the spur are beveled at an angle of 8°; on most spade bits the lips are perpendicular to the axis of the bit, but in some they are set at an angle. On a dull spade bit the bevels are slightly rounded and the cutting lips slightly unequal and out of line.

An auger bit. A central screw point draws the auger bit into the wood; at the edge of the hole, spurs score the wood ahead of the cutting lips, which cut wood within the scored circle. The twisted throat carries chips out of the hole.

The bit should be sharpened when the edges of the spurs and cutting lips are dull or chipped. The spurs should project far enough to score the wood fibers thoroughly before the cutting lips make contact; the lips should be equal in length and beveled in the same plane.

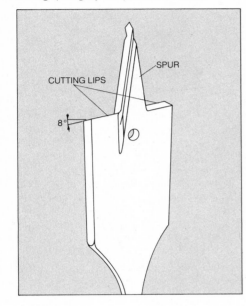

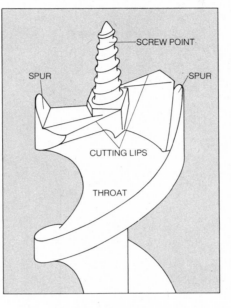

Grinding a Twist Bit

1 Setting up a guide block. Use a T bevel and a pencil to draw a line across the tool rest of the grinding wheel at an angle to the face of the wheel that is half of the correct angle for the bit tip—for most twist bits, set the T bevel to 59°; for special wood bits, to 41°. To the left of this line, at ¼-inch intervals, lay out several parallel lines at an angle 12° less than the first—usually this will be a 47° angle. Use a C clamp to secure a small block of wood to the tool rest, at the right of and flush with the 59° line.

For twist bits smaller than ⅛ inch, omit the parallel lines but adjust the tool rest so that the back edge is 12° lower than the front edge.

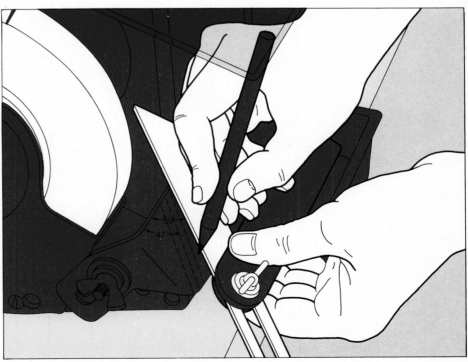

2 Grinding the bit. Wearing safety goggles or a face mask, start the motor and let the grinding wheel run until it reaches a steady speed. Hold the shank of the twist bit in your right hand and use your left to position the bit against the guide block with one cutting lip perfectly horizontal. Slowly move the bit forward until it makes contact with the wheel, then simultaneously rotate the shank of the bit clockwise and swing the entire bit parallel to the 47° lines. Time the movements so that when the bit reaches the 49° position you have rolled from the cutting lip to the heel of a point surface *(inset)*.

Position the bit with the other cutting lip horizontal and grind the second point surface in the same way. Alternate the passes between the point surfaces, grinding each equally until the bit is sharp. After each two or three passes, stop to cool the bit.

Position a bit smaller than ⅛ inch in the same way, but do not swing or rotate the bit.

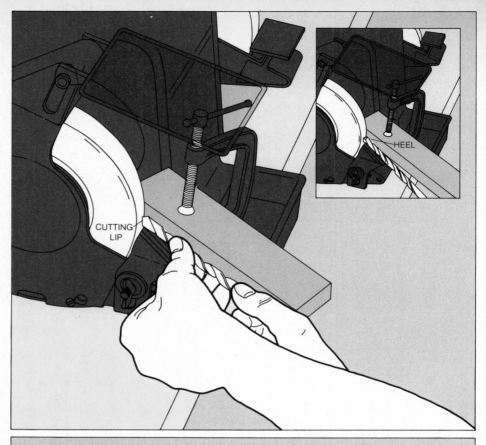

CUTTING LIP

HEEL

3 Checking the bit. Set the bit in the lip corner of a drill gauge to compare the lengths of the cutting lips, then turn the bit slightly to check the clearance at the heels *(inset)*. If the lips or clearances are unequal, regrind the bit.

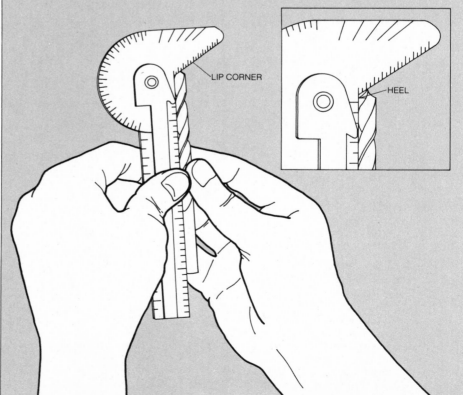

LIP CORNER

HEEL

Correcting the Bevel of a Spade Bit

Grinding the edge bevels. Set the tool rest at an angle of 8° to the horizontal, with the higher end facing the grinding wheel, and tighten a stop collar on the shank of a spade bit so that when the stop bears against the edge of the rest, the bit's cutting lips will bear against the wheel face. Hold the bit flat on the tool rest and apply a cutting lip, bevel facing down, to the wheel face. When one lip has been ground, flip the bit to grind the other lip. To grind the bevels at the edges of the spur, swing the bit about 90° and guide it against the wheel freehand *(inset)*. Flip the bit to grind the opposite spur edge, taking care to grind both edges equally so that the spur remains centered.

Remove burrs on the spurs and lips with one or two light strokes of a whetstone on the flat faces.

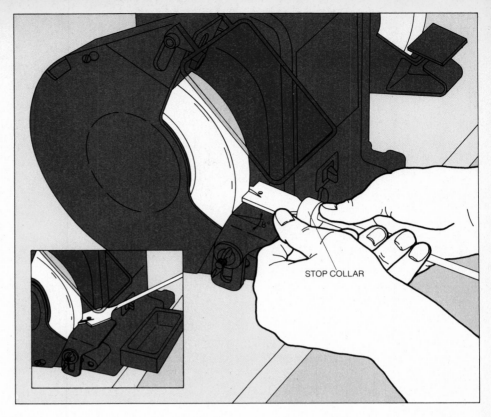

STOP COLLAR

Filing Auger Bits and Countersinks

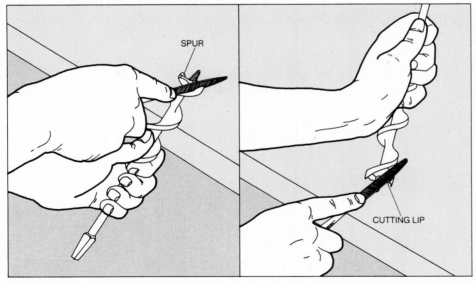

SPUR

CUTTING LIP

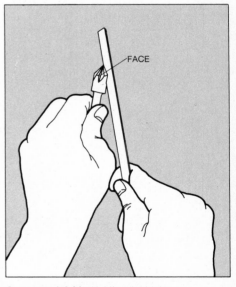

FACE

An auger bit. Hold the throat of the bit against the edge of a worktable so that the cutting head projects above the table, and make straight, even, pushing strokes with an auger-bit file to sharpen the inside edge of each spur *(left)*. Do not file the outsides of the spurs, as this will reduce the size of the hole that the head bores and cause the shaft of the bit to bind. Rest the head of the bit on the worktable and file the top of the cut-

ting lips to a sharp edge beveled at about 45° *(right)*. Take special care to file bevels that are equal in length and angle, and be sure that you do not undercut the base of the screw point. Do not file the underside of the cutting lips, next to the screw point.

To complete the job, lightly whet the filed edges with an auger-bit whetstone.

A countersink bit. Holding the bit in your hand, use a small triangular whetstone to sharpen the faces of the fluted cutting edges with light, even strokes; take special care to keep the stone flat against each face. Do not sharpen the backs of the cutting edges, as this may alter their height so that they will not cut, but complete the job by removing the burr from each back with a single, light stroke of the stone.

3

The Knack of Shaping Wood

Planes that smooth curves. Spokeshaves, miniature variations of the everyday plane, are made with soles, or base plates, so short that they can follow tight curves—here the curved edges of decorative cornice braces. The spokeshave at top has a flat sole, for convex curves and for some narrow straight cuts such as the chamfer shown on page 89; the one at bottom has a slightly rounded sole, for concave surfaces.

Wood has always been special—spirits were said to live in it, and other gods and demigods were said to protect the trees that produced it. In part, this special reverence stems from the many uses of wood, from buildings to bowls, but certainly another reason must be the elegance and simplicity with which wood achieves these practical ends. It can be shaped into graceful forms. Its edges can be smoothed to meet for a seemingly seamless corner, or they can be shaped to lock in a grip that will endure over the centuries.

Of the hundreds of such jointing techniques that once were essential to the house carpenter's work, only a few remain in common use: miters, which fit trim around angles; kerfing, which flexes boards for curves; rabbets and dadoes, two related shapes used for joints; and mortises and tenons, which lock joints in moving assemblies such as windows and doors. All are ancient, still known by their old names. And ironically, most are created today either by one of the oldest of tools, the plane, or by one of the newest, the router. The two tools are dissimilar. The plane (as well as its variant, the spokeshave) is a blade in a holder. The router is a spinning bit.

The plane is often the symbol of a woodworker's highest craftsmanship, not only for what it can do but also for its beauty as a tool. As early as the Roman era, the plane was a sophisticated instrument, and in Baroque times it flourished into a wide range of shapes and sizes to carve the moldings for lavish palaces. By the 18th Century, woodworkers made a separate plane for every wood shape, from delicate beading to structural joints.

The tools themselves were reverenced. Each workman made his own, fashioning each to fit his grip. With his plane the woodworker used his eye, his ear, but most of all his hands, and when he used it he had what admirers called the knack—the precise art of forming wood to the perfect shape, whether for a rabbet joint in a Quaker doorjamb or the fluted pilaster astride a Georgian window.

The whisper of a plane is now often replaced by the whir of a router. Electric motors and toughened steel led the way to speed in fashioning wood. And the router bit cuts so smoothly that it simultaneously shapes and finishes, making sanding almost superfluous.

Yet even in the machine age, using the plane and the router calls for skills. Both tools require adjustments so precise that only the eye can serve as arbiter. With both tools the worker needs to know how hard to press against the wood and how fast to push along the fibers. Tools do not have the knack: craftsmen do. Once achieved, the knack leads to some of the most beautiful results in woodworking: a shape that perfectly fits its function, a look of warmth and rhythm, and a feel that only fingers can sense is truly smooth.

Planing a Board to Lie Flat and Fit Tight

For trimming and smoothing wood, no tool is more accurate than a hand plane with a razor-sharp blade. It is the ideal tool for such jobs as leveling a surface for a porch step; shaving an edge, such as the narrow top of a drawer; or, by using a technique called "shooting" *(page 84)*, shaping the edge of a board exactly perpendicular to its face.

A hand plane's major shortcoming is its reliance on muscle power; on big jobs, such as smoothing the faces of large boards or trimming doors, you may want to speed and ease the work with a portable power plane *(page 87)*.

Ordinary jobs are handled by two types of hand planes—two-hand bench planes and smaller, simpler, one-hand block planes. Bench planes come in a variety of sizes, but all have the same basic design. The blade, called an iron, is mounted about 45° from the horizontal with its bevel side down; it protrudes through a slit called the mouth, in the bottom, or sole. As the plane moves forward, the blade pries up a thin shaving that is lifted and curled by a second iron, called the cap iron, which has a rounded "nose" rather than a cutting edge.

The depth of the cutting blade, its distance from the front of the mouth, and its position with respect to the cap-iron nose determine exactly how the wood is cut. The most versatile of the bench planes is the 14-inch jack plane, long and heavy enough for straightening edges and leveling surfaces, yet light enough for smoothing, a job requiring many fine, careful strokes.

The block plane is a one-hand tool originally designed for smoothing butcher blocks made by piecing together short boards, end grain up. Still the tool of choice for small end-grain jobs, the block plane is also used for light trimming and for smoothing plywood edges. To crosscut the exposed fibers of an end grain, the iron is set at a lower angle to the wood than that of a bench plane, and the bevel of the cutting edge faces upward. A good block plane has an adjustable blade depth and mouth opening, and a lateral-adjusting lever *(page 86)*.

Whatever plane you use, follow these general rules: Cut with the grain wherever possible, to avoid tearing the wood fiber; if the grain changes direction along the length of a board, change the direction of your stroke. Let the feel of the plane skimming the wood be a guide: planing should never be hard work. If you plane against the grain, you will im-mediately feel a roughness and hardness in the cut. When planing faces or broad edges, jobs in which the entire sole is in contact with the wood, rub paraffin on the sole to reduce friction.

When you finish planing or are interrupted in the course of a job, set the plane on its side to avoid damaging the iron. Test the trueness of a planed surface by placing a straightedge, a combination square or the factory-cut edge of a length of plywood on your board. If light shows between the board and the straightedge, mark the high spots with a pencil, then plane off your markings.

Although hand planes are relatively simple tools, they are intricately assembled from a number of parts, each with its own distinctive name. Before using a hand plane, remove the iron and familiarize yourself with the parts. The lever cap secures the iron and cap iron in place; all three rest on an angled support called the frog; screws and levers change the depth of the blade, tilt it, or move it forward and back. With the plane disassembled, sharpen the iron *(pages 102-107)* until it can easily slice through the edge of a piece of paper held in one hand. Then reassemble the parts, taking special care in the precise adjustment of the blade.

The Parts of a Bench Plane

1 **Assembling the iron and cap iron.** Screw the knurled cap screw lightly into the cap iron, then hold the iron, bevel side down, at right angles to the cap iron, slip the head of the cap screw through the hole at the end of the slot of the iron and slide the cap iron at least halfway along the slot. Rotate the cap iron until the sides of the two irons align—make sure the front of the cap iron does not scrape across the iron's cutting edge. For general work on wood that is fairly easy to cut, such as pine, slide the cap iron forward gently until the front of its nose is about 1/16 inch from the edge of the blade. Tighten the cap screw with your fingers, then give it an additional quarter turn with a screwdriver. For wood that is more difficult to cut, such as oak, or for finishing work, advance the cap iron 1/32 inch closer to the cutting edge.

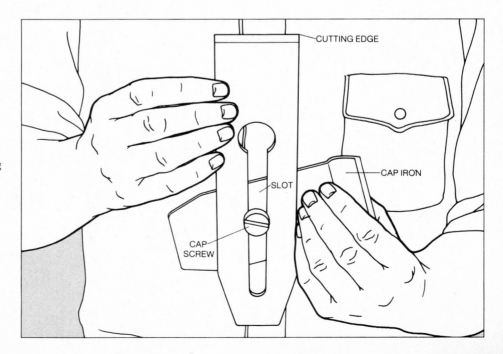

2 Installing the irons. Insert the blade into the mouth of the plane, fit the irons over the lever-cap screw, and lay the irons on the frog—the top of the depth-adjusting lug should fit into the window in the cap iron and the lateral-adjusting roller should fit into the iron's slot. Set the lever cap on the irons, slide it down until the narrow portion of its hole fits around the lever-cap screw, and snap the lever-cap cam down. The cam should snap down with moderate thumb pressure. If it does not go, release the cam and either loosen the lever-cap screw to decrease tension or tighten it to increase tension.

3 Setting the depth of the blade. Hold the plane upright, with the heel resting on a light-colored surface and the sole facing away from you. Sighting down the sole, turn the depth-adjusting nut until the blade barely protrudes through the mouth; if the blade protrudes farther at one side of the mouth than at the other, use the lateral-adjusting lever to even it.

The mechanical link between the depth-adjusting nut and the depth-adjusting lug has a small amount of play. Be certain that the final adjustment of the nut moves the blade deeper through the mouth: otherwise the blade will slide back slightly during the first stroke.

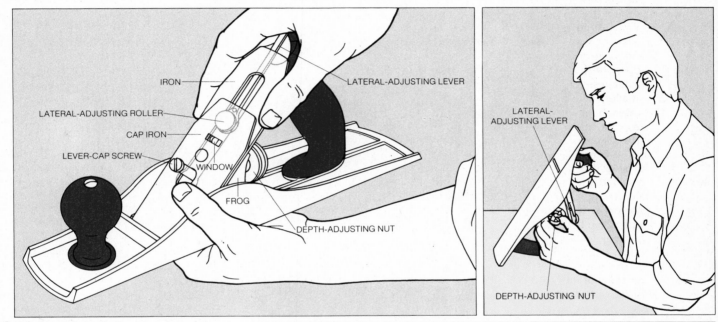

IRON
LATERAL-ADJUSTING LEVER
LATERAL-ADJUSTING ROLLER
CAP IRON
LEVER-CAP SCREW
WINDOW
FROG
DEPTH-ADJUSTING NUT

LATERAL-ADJUSTING LEVER
DEPTH-ADJUSTING NUT

4 Adjusting the mouth. Turn the sole toward you to check the mouth width. For easy-to-cut wood, use a wide opening; for harder material use a narrow opening (the inset shows the correct widths, actual size). If the opening is too wide or too narrow, remove the lever cap and the irons, exposing two screws called bed screws in the frog. Loosen these screws, then retract or advance the frog-adjusting screw—only a slight adjustment should be needed. Reassemble the plane, check the mouth opening again, and test it with a scrap of wood.

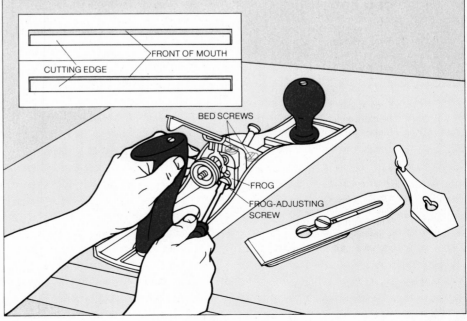

FRONT OF MOUTH
CUTTING EDGE
BED SCREWS
FROG
FROG-ADJUSTING SCREW

Working with the Plane

Planing an edge. Secure the board between two pieces of wood in a vise. Place one hand on the rear handle of the plane, set the toe of the plane squarely on the end of the board and prepare to guide the strokes by curling the other hand around the side of the plane so that your thumb rests near the knob, your fingertips touch the sole just ahead of the blade and the backs of your fingers will brush the board beneath the plane. (If the wood is splintery, you may have to forego this method and instead guide the plane by placing your forward hand on the knob of the plane.)

Begin the first pass with slightly more pressure on the toe than on the heel. Allow pressure to shift naturally on the plane so that pressure is even in the middle of the pass. To be sure that the sole runs flat on the board edge when the blade hits the corner at the end of the stroke, apply slightly more pressure there on the heel.

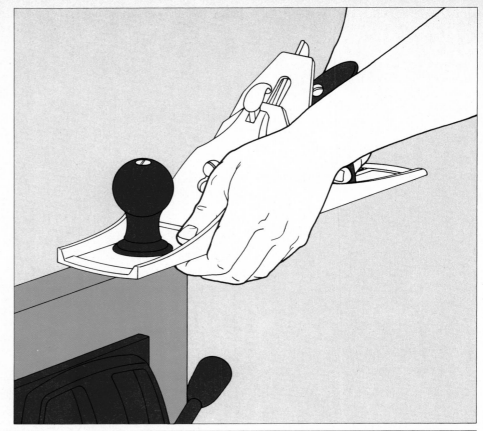

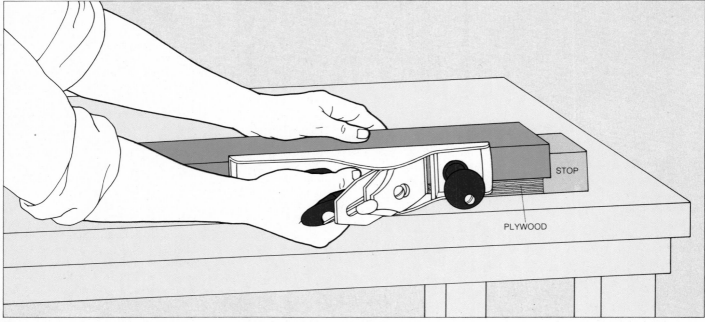

"Shooting" a right angle. To plane the edge of a board perpendicular to its face, place the board on a flat piece of plywood, with the edge of the board overlapping the edge of the plywood by about ⅛ inch; butt the plywood and the board against a stop fastened to the workbench. Hold the board and the plywood firmly against the stop with one hand, lay the plane, set for a fine shaving, on its side on the workbench and plane toward the stop. Your cuts will result in a perfect right angle since the sole and sides of a plane are milled to meet at 90° angles. Note: If you find it difficult to hold the board steady against a single stop, you may prefer to secure both ends of the board and the plywood base with stops. To shoot several boards in succession, build a permanent shooting board similar to the miter shooting board shown on page 90, but cut the plywood as long as your boards and substitute a perpendicular stop on one end for the mitered stop.

Planing end grain. Secure the board, end grain up, in a vise, along with a piece of scrap to extend the planing surface beyond the edge of the board. If possible, clamp the scrap to the board so that the planing action cannot cause the two to separate. With the blade set for a very fine cut, place the plane flat on the board as you would in planing an edge, but place the plane itself at about a 30° angle with the board. Plane along the board end, holding the plane at the 30° angle to slice through the tough end grain, and continue the strokes onto the scrap.

If you cannot fit scrap into the vise, plane about three fourths of the way across the end grain; then, after a few passes, reverse direction by starting the strokes at the opposite side of the board and planing toward, but not over, the portion you have already planed.

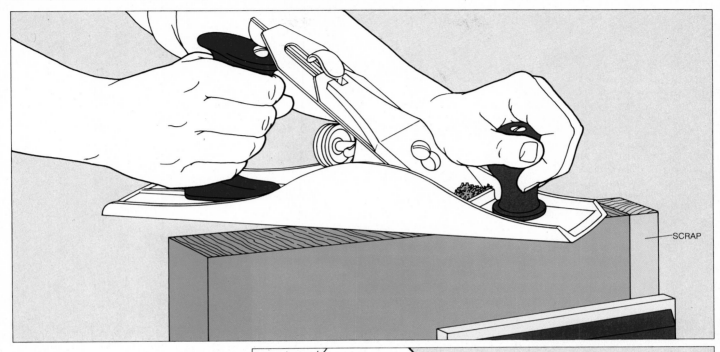

SCRAP

Planing a face. Secure the board between two stops on a workbench, and plane the face in two stages, first for leveling, then for smoothing. In the first stage, set the blade for cuts about as deep as the thickness of an index card, hold the plane at an angle of about 45° to the grain and make straight, slightly overlapping strokes with the edge of the blade at right angles to the direction of the strokes. Before beginning the smoothing stage, resharpen the iron and set the blade for tissue-thin shavings; plane the face with straight strokes parallel to the grain.

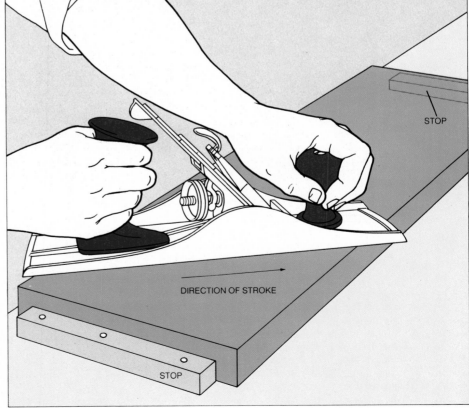

STOP

DIRECTION OF STROKE

STOP

Working with a Block Plane

Adjusting the plane. Hold the plane in one hand and use the other to insert the iron, bevel up, fit the lever cap over the iron and tighten the locking lever. Turn the plane upside down so that you can sight along the sole, then set the depth of the blade with the depth-adjusting nut and set the blade parallel to the sole with the lateral-adjusting lever. For trimming edges on easier-to-cut woods, loosen the finger-rest screw and open the mouth to about $1/16$ inch by shifting the mouth-adjusting lever; for end grain, for harder-to-cut woods and for plywood, close the mouth to about $1/32$ inch.

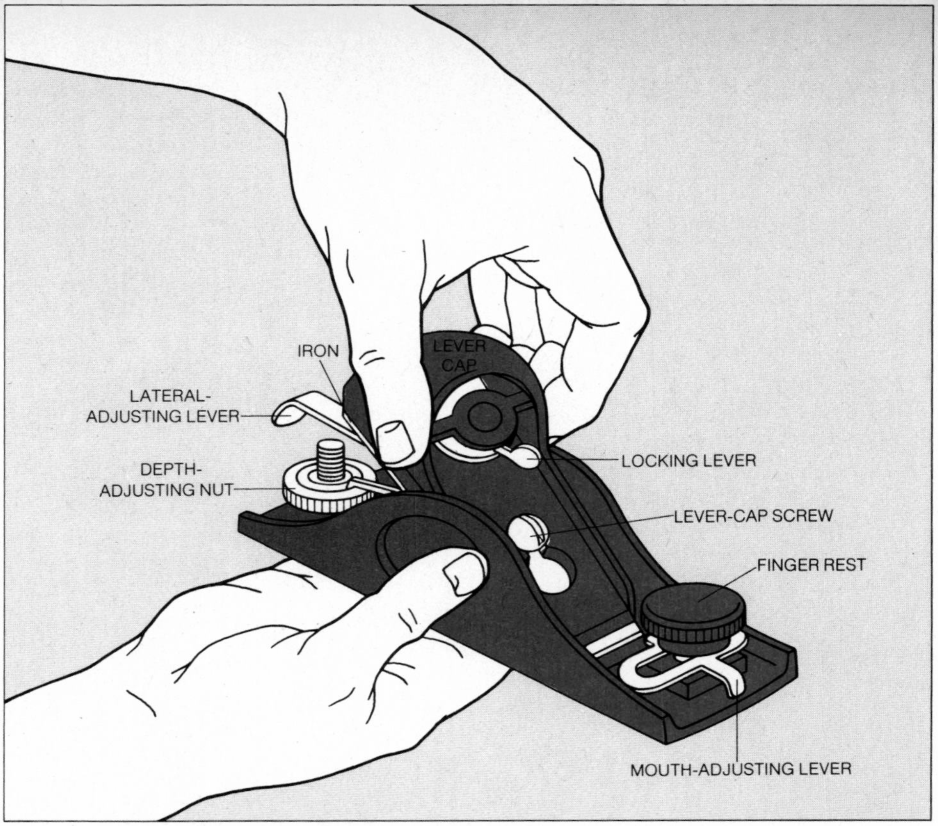

Trimming the wood. Hold the block plane in one hand with your palm on the lever cap, your index finger on the finger rest, and your thumb and fingers on the sides. Begin each stroke with slightly more pressure on the toe, and finish it with slightly more pressure on the heel.

Small chips of wood rather than shavings should rise from end grain and plywood. If the plane "chatters"—that is, vibrates—and is hard to push, adjust the blade upward for a shallower cut.

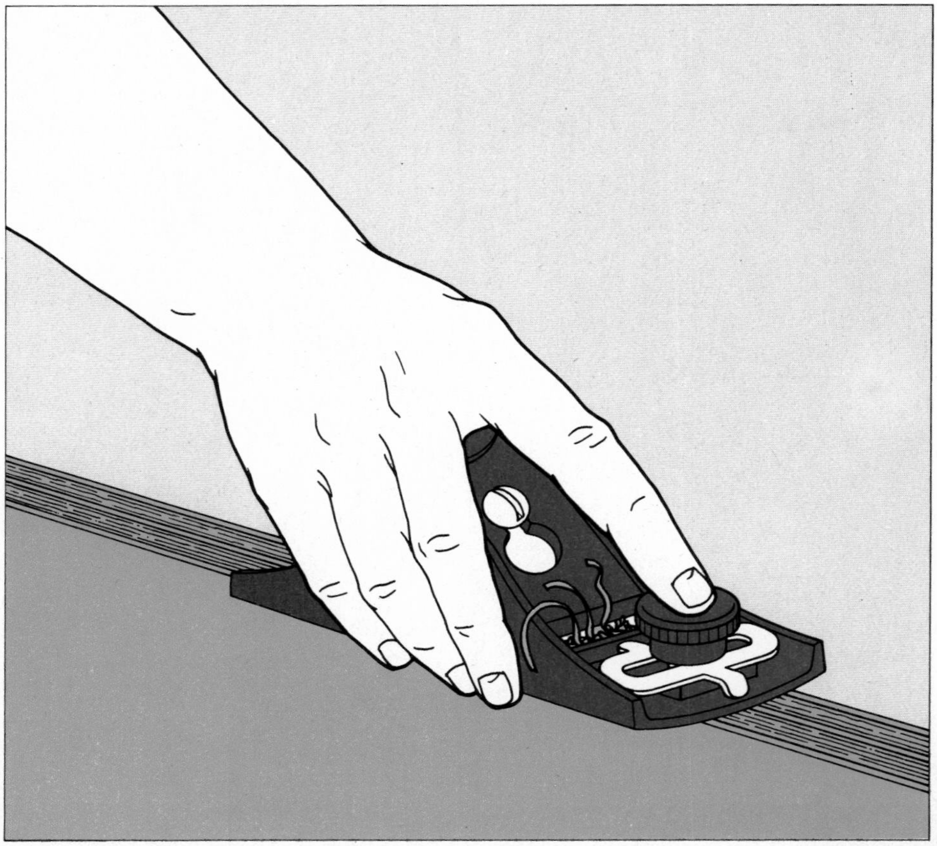

LATERAL-ADJUSTING LEVER

DEPTH-ADJUSTING NUT

IRON

LEVER CAP

LOCKING LEVER

LEVER-CAP SCREW

FINGER REST

MOUTH-ADJUSTING LEVER

For Big Jobs: A Power Planer

Portable power planes range from small one-hand block planes to 10-pound bench planes, and many come with such accessories as fences and brackets for making square edges and accurate bevels, but all work in much the same way. A rotating drum turns at speeds up to 25,000 revolutions per minute, shearing away wood fiber through the mouth of the plane. Unlike hand planes, power planes can easily cut across the grain and even against the grain; nevertheless, plane with the grain for best results.

The only adjustment needed on a power plane is depth of the cut, generally regulated by a knob that raises or lowers the toe, which is independent of the rest of the sole; the depth of the blades themselves never changes. In most models, the maximum recommended cutting depth is about 1/16 of an inch, a depth suitable for work on rough wood.

Safety Tips for Power Planers

☐ Fasten the wood securely—in a vise, with clamps, or between strong stops fastened to a workbench.
☐ Keep both your hands on the handles of the plane at all times. Never curl your fingers under the sole to guide the plane.
☐ Never set the plane down at the end of a job until the motor has stopped completely.

Setting depth of the cut. With the cord unplugged, turn the adjusting knob; typically, a full turn of the knob raises or lowers the blade about 1/16 inch. The manufacturer's instructions generally recommend specific depths of cut for various jobs, but make trial cuts on scrap to be sure you have the depth you need.

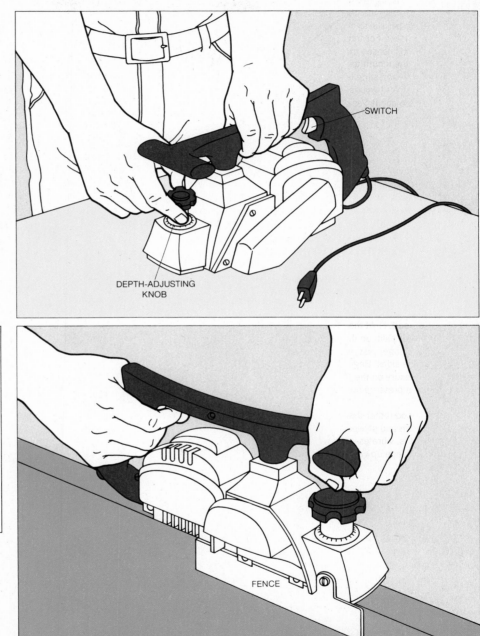

SWITCH

DEPTH-ADJUSTING KNOB

FENCE

Making the cut. Gripping both handles firmly, place the toe of the plane on the board; start the motor while the blades are still clear and let it reach maximum speed before beginning the cut. Move the plane forward steadily, using more pressure on the toe at the beginning of the cut, and on the heel at the end. For smoother cuts, move the plane forward more slowly.

For such jobs as beveling or, as in this example, planing the edge of a door, attach a fence to the plane to guide the cut.

Shaving and Shaping to Angles and Curves

Although most boards in a house are squared off all around, some trim pieces are not. Giving them their final shapes requires special techniques and, in a few cases, special tools. A door edge, for example, is planed to a slanted bevel across the entire width of the edge so that the door closes easily.

A plane, or its relative a spokeshave (opposite), shapes most edges. Ends cut to a 45° angle for a miter joint may need to be planed to shorten them or to smooth them for a perfect fit, particularly if the joint will have a clear finish and imperfections cannot be hidden by wood filler and paint. This precise planing is simplified with a homemade jig called a miter shooting board (page 90, top). Also, sharp-edged corners—especially on posts—are relieved by planing just the corner, rather than the entire edge, into a "chamfer." A decorative variant of the chamfer running only partway along the edge is cut with a spokeshave.

A spokeshave also finishes edges that curve, although a rasp or sandpaper often can serve. For some curved pieces—a curving section of baseboard or a jamb for an arched doorway—a special procedure must be used to bend a board so that its face curves.

To shape entire boards into a curve, professionals usually bend several thin boards in a large press and glue them together to form a single laminated board of the desired curvature. This technique requires equipment seldom available to amateurs. However, if the piece is less than 1 inch thick, you can bend stock lumber by cutting closely spaced saw kerfs partway through the back, then bending and nailing the board around a curved base. Though a kerfed board can be bent around a shallow inside curve—such as the rounded corner of a room—by flexing the kerfs open, the board will bend much farther around an outside curve like that on page 90.

The kerfs that permit bending a board face will show on the edges of the board, and there is no way to conceal them that is both easy and completely satisfactory. Many carpenters fill the edge cuts with wood filler, then sand the edge—a fairly simple job on the squared edge of an arch jamb, but difficult on a baseboard, which should have a shaped edge. This problem can be avoided in the case of a baseboard if the curve required is shallow: use plain, unshaped stock for the curving baseboard, then cover the cut edge by nailing to it quarter-round or ogee molding, which is flexible enough to bend somewhat without kerfing.

For a board to be bent in this way, use straight, clear lumber, free of knots and cracks. Woods with long fibers—oak, pine and fir, for example—can be bent easily with this method; woods with shorter fibers, such as cherry and mahogany, are stiffer and cannot be bent into extremely tight curves.

Making Bevels and Chamfers with a Bench Plane

Freehand planing at an angle. Using a T bevel (page 28), mark the angle of the bevel across the end of the board, then use a marking gauge (page 22) to scribe a line for the bottom of the bevel along the face of the board. Plane the bevel as you would a square edge (page 84), but tilt the sole of the plane roughly parallel to the line on the end of the board. As the plane nears the corner of the board at one face and the line on the opposite face, adjust the angle of the sole precisely, so that you reach both simultaneously. Check the angle of the completed bevel with a T bevel and a straightedge, mark any high spots and shave them down.

To flatten a sharp corner over its full length for a "through" chamfer (inset), mark the angle (usually 45°) on the end of the board and scribe matching lines on both the face and the edge, then plane the angle as you would a bevel. To make a "stopped" chamfer, which does not run the full length of the corner, use a spokeshave as described on the opposite page.

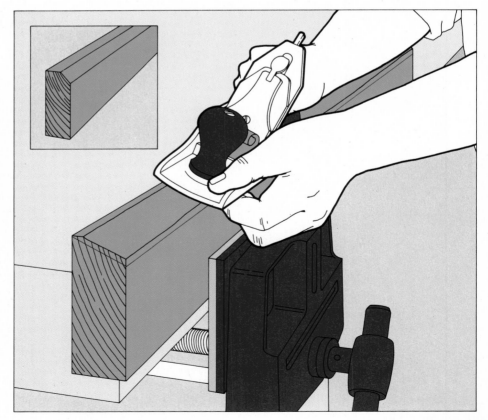

Smoothing Decorative Trim with a Spokeshave

Anatomy of a spokeshave. The parts of a spokeshave fit together in the same way as those of a bench plane, but the spokeshave's short sole—flat for straight and convex shapes, rounded for concave ones—allows it to plane curved surfaces. The blade, beveled like that of a plane iron *(page 82)*, fits into the body of the spokeshave with its bevel side down. The depth and angle of the blade can be adjusted with flanged nuts that are set in notches in the upper corners of the blade. The blade is held down by an iron lever-cap like that of a plane; the fulcrum of the lever is the locking screw that fastens the cap to the body of the spokeshave. The lever-cap can be tightened by a knurled thumbscrew that presses against the top of the blade, forcing together the bottom edge of the cap and the bottom of the blade.

To adjust the blade, tighten the locking screw until it is barely snug, turn the adjusting nuts until the cutting edge of the blade barely projects below the sole, then tighten the thumbscrew firmly by hand. Check the depth adjustment by making trial shavings with a scrap of wood; the wood shavings should be tissue-thin. If the spokeshave vibrates and chops at the wood, reset the blade to a shallower depth.

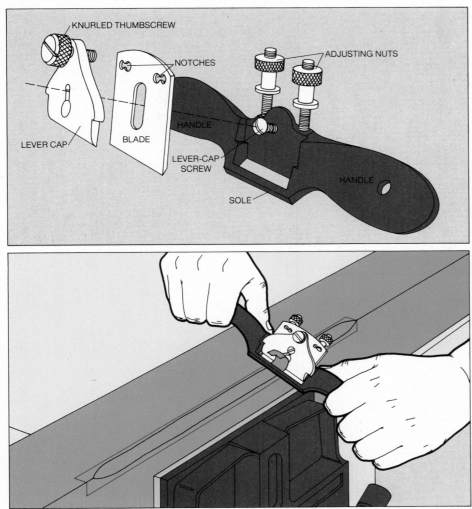

Making a stopped chamfer. Use a pencil to mark the ends of the chamfer and a marking gauge to mark the chamfer lines on the edge and face of the board. Sighting through the mouth, set a flat-bottomed spokeshave on the mark at one end of the chamfer, with the handles tilted 45° from the horizontal, and push the spokeshave forward with the grain to a point about ⅛ inch from the other end. After every two or three passes along the entire length of the chamfer, make a short cut at the far end to pare away the shavings. Shave the chamfer down to the marked lines, then set the blade on the mark at the far end of the chamfer and shave the stop to a smooth, gradual curve that matches the one you made at the starting point.

Smoothing a curve. Clamp the board—in this example, a curved piece of gingerbread trim—in a vise with the grain running horizontally. Set a spokeshave at the top of a curve and push it slowly to the bottom, using a round-bottomed spokeshave for a concave curve *(above)* and a flat-bottomed spokeshave for a convex curve. Then reverse direction and push the spokeshave down from the other side of the curve; work back and forth until the surface is smooth. Do not push the spokeshave uphill, against the grain; it will gouge and chip the surface.

A Shooting Board
for Miter Cuts

Building a shooting board. Designed to assist in accurate planing at an angle, this jig has an 18-by-12-inch base of ¾-inch plywood, to which is screwed an 18-by-9-inch shelf and a trapezoidal stop. For one long side of the shelf, use the straight, factory-cut edge of the plywood, and attach the shelf so that this straight edge is the side stepped back from the base.

For the stop, cut a 9-inch rectangle of plywood, then, using a miter box, cut its ends in two opposing 45° angles about 2 inches apart. Set the stop on top of the shelf, its 2-inch side flush with the factory-cut edge. Check its angled sides with a combination square and move the stop until they form exact 45° angles with the factory-cut edge, then screw the stop in place.

Planing the miter. Hold the board firmly against one side of the stop, with the mitered end about 1/32 inch beyond the edge of the stop. Adjust a jack plane for a very fine cut *(page 83, Step 3)* and rest it on its side with its toe against the miter. Slide the plane forward repeatedly, starting each stroke with the toe against the miter and stopping it when the blade passes the miter—planing farther will plane the trapezoid and ruin its straight edge. As you shave the miter down, edge the board forward so that it always protrudes about 1/32 inch beyond the stop. If the plane becomes hard to push, rub paraffin on the shooting board and the side of the plane.

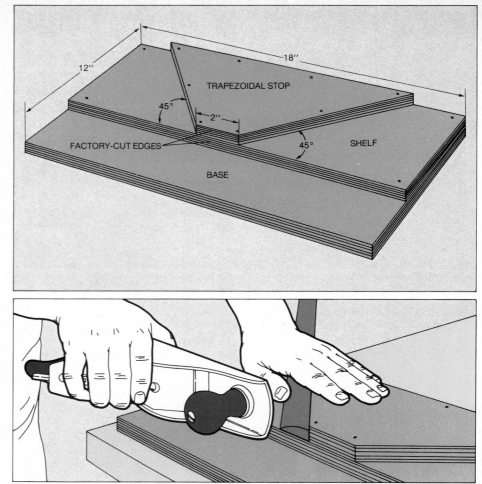

Bending a Board
with the Help of a Saw

1 **Measuring the curve.** Hold a straightedge at each end of the curve and mark the spring lines where the curve begins *(page 50, Step 2)*. Measure the distance between the spring lines with a flexible steel tape and transfer these measurements to the board you will bend; provide as much unbent wood at each end of the board as is practical—no less than 6 inches.

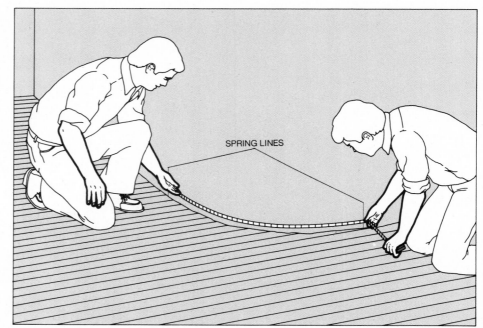

2 Cutting the kerfs. You will have to experiment to find the correct depth and spacing of the kerfs for your particular curve and type of wood. If you use a radial arm saw, start by marking the fence ½ inch from the right side of the blade and setting the blade depth ⅛ inch above the saw table. In a 2-foot scrap that matches the one you plan to bend, cut kerfs at ½-inch intervals (*pages 14-21*), aligning each new kerf with the mark on the fence for the correct spacing.

Bend the kerfed scrap around a section of the curve to test its flexibility. If you hear cracking in the board or if you must strain to bend it, make trial cuts in other scraps, gradually increasing the depth of the cuts and decreasing the space between them until you find the minimum depth and maximum spacing that permits the necessary bend. However, to avoid serious weakening of the wood, you must leave at least $\frac{1}{16}$ inch of uncut wood and space the kerfs at least ¼ inch apart. Use the depth and spacing measurements that you determined in the trials on scrap to make kerfs between the spring lines in the back of the board you plan to bend.

If you use a portable circular saw to cut the kerfs, guide it with the jig shown on page 17, bottom; or mark a line on the board for each kerf, allowing ⅛ inch for the width of the saw blade, and cut the kerfs freehand.

3 Nailing the kerfed board. While a helper holds the board—in this example, a section of baseboard—bent around the curve, nail the straight section at one end in the usual way, then drill pilot holes every 8 inches through the uncut wood between kerfs and into the sole plate. Fasten with sixpenny finishing nails.

To conceal the kerfs exposed at the edge of the board, fill them with wood filler.

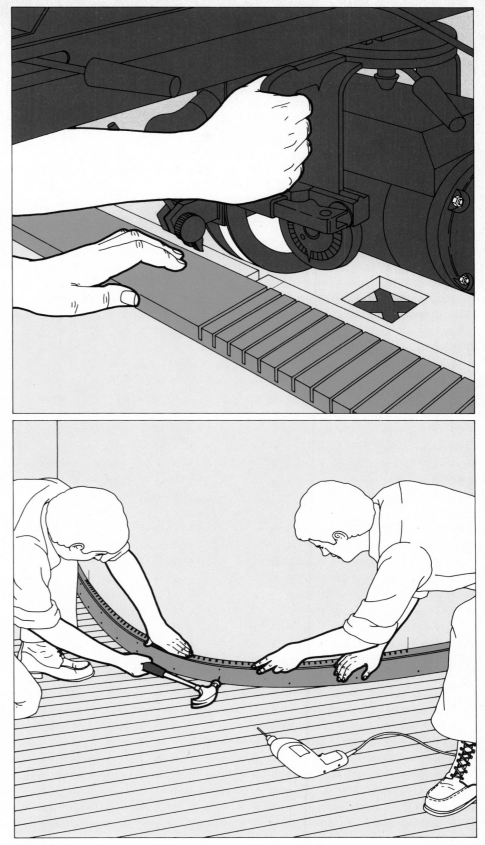

Notches: Rough Passageways and Smooth Joints

A multitude of notches must be cut in the rough frame of a house for the pipes and cables that will run behind the walls and ceilings of the finished rooms. Since most of these notches are made in studs or joists that will later be concealed, you can fashion them roughly—typically by making preliminary cuts with a circular saw, then chopping away the wood. The ideal chopping tools are chisels with ¾-inch to 1½-inch beveled blades and steel-capped handles.

Though the notches are made by simple techniques, their planning and placement are anything but simple. Cutting into a framing member weakens it, and a notch in a board that supports weight—for example, a stud in a bearing wall—must conform to the prescriptions of your local building codes. Check the codes when you plan a notch—and do not be surprised if you find it difficult to meet their prescriptions literally.

A building code, for example, may prohibit a notch larger than 2 inches square, while the outside diameter of a pipe measures 2½ inches. Building inspectors will generally allow a larger notch if you reinforce the stud. In most cases, a small steel plate called a kickplate *(opposite, center),* placed over the notch to protect its pipe or cable from nails, may meet the legal requirements. If it does not, you must notch larger steel plates into the stud following the same method you use to recess a kickplate.

While precision cutting is unnecessary for notches in rough framing, it is neces-sary for notches that serve as parts of finished joints—the mortise-and-tenon joints at the corners of doors or windows, for example *(pages 132-133).* Tenon notches, which must be measured and cut precisely, are generally made on the ends of the shorter boards in the joint—boards that are easier to handle and to fix in a vise for cutting.

To match a tenon to the width, length and depth of a mortise, you must cut the end of the board with a backsaw to form a notch with perpendicular shoulders, and smooth the corners between the notch and the shoulders with a chisel. When the joint is completed and assembled, the squared shoulders of the tenon will fit flush against the wood at the sides of the mortise.

Notching the Frame of a House

A shallow V notch in an edge. Turn the bevel of a chisel toward the notch and drive the chisel into the wood at a 45° angle to cut one side; then reverse the bevel to chisel in toward the bottom of the first cut, forming the second side. The wood will chip out of the notch as you cut.

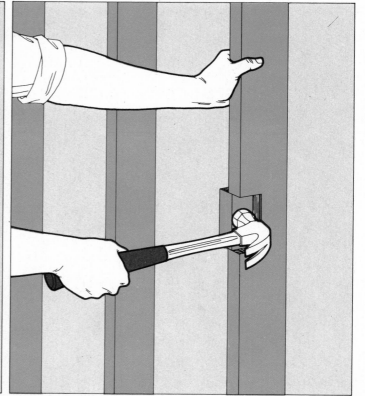

A deep notch in an edge. Set the blade of a circular saw to the depth of the planned notch and make two cuts across the edge of the board to outline the notch; then, with a hammer, strike between the saw cuts to knock out the waste wood with a single sharp blow.

Notching a board face. With a circular saw set to depth of the desired notch, make parallel cuts across the face at each side of the notch and also at approximately ¼-inch intervals between the sides. Secure the board, edge up, in a vise. Set the cutting edge of the chisel parallel to the grain and across the inner ends of the saw cuts, with the bevel facing the cuts; then hammer the chisel across the board.

Recessing for a kickplate. Hold a steel kickplate, which may be needed to protect cable or piping in a face or edge notch, over the notch and score the wood at the ends of the plate with a utility knife. Set a chisel perpendicular to the board at each score line, with the bevel facing the notch, and tap the chisel ⅛ inch deep into the wood *(near right)*. To remove the waste wood, set the chisel ⅛ inch inside the existing notch, with the bevel facing outward, and drive it to the end of the recess *(far right)*.

A shallow end notch. Secure the board, edge up, in a vise and outline the notch on the edge, the face and the end of the board. Using a circular saw set to the depth of the notch, cut down across the edge of the board at the marked line; place the chisel blade, bevel up, at the mark on the end of the board and drive the chisel horizontally toward the saw cut.

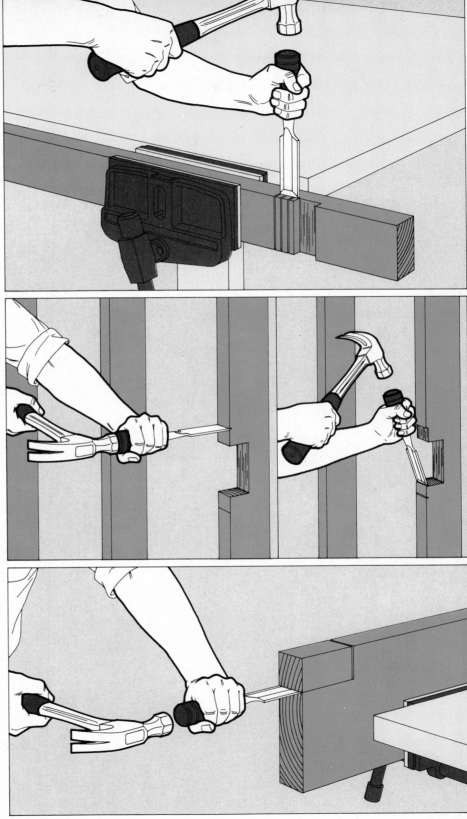

A deep end notch. If the depth of a notch exceeds the maximum depth setting of your circular saw, use the circular saw to cut along marks on the board face as far as the inner corner of the notch. To cut the corner on the underside of the board, where the circular-saw blade did not reach, slide a handsaw into each circular-saw kerf and, holding the cutting edge of the blade vertical, saw the rest of the way to the corner.

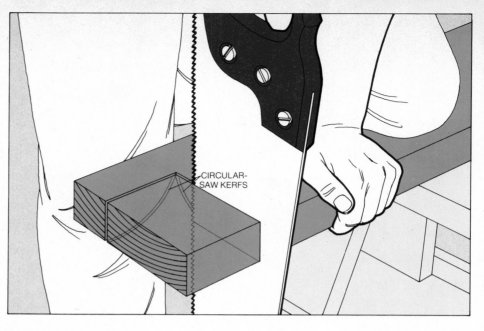

CIRCULAR-
SAW KERFS

A Set of Precise Notches for a Tenon

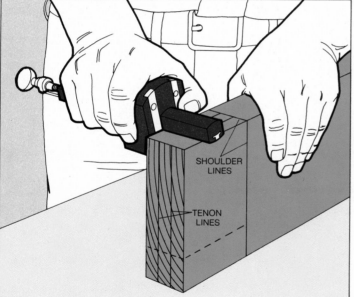

SHOULDER
LINES

TENON
LINES

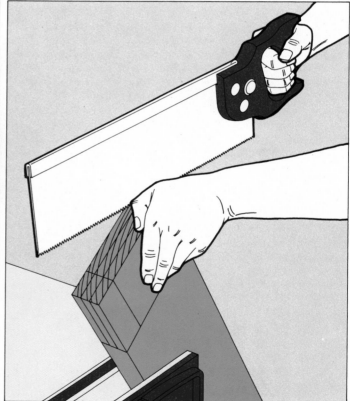

1 Marking the outlines. Use a combination square and a sharp utility knife to score so-called shoulder lines across the faces and edges of the board at a distance from the end equal to the depth of the mortise minus ⅛ inch. Next, use a mortising gauge (pages 132-133) to score two parallel lines called tenon lines on the end of the board as far apart as the width of the mortise and to extend the tenon lines along the edges of the board to meet the shoulder lines. With a utility knife, score a line across the end of the board, perpendicular to the scored tenon lines, to mark off the length of the tenon; extend the line down both faces of the board as far as the shoulder lines.

2 Starting the tenon-line cuts. Secure the board at about a 60° angle in a woodworking vise, position a backsaw at a 45° angle to the edge of the board and saw along the waste side of each tenon line until the kerf reaches the shoulder line. Turn the board over and cut the tenon lines on the other edge in the same way.

3 Completing the tenon-line cuts. Secure the board vertically, set the saw into the diagonal kerfs of each tenon line and, keeping the blade horizontal, saw down to the shoulder lines. Then set the saw across the end of the board on the line that marks the length of the tenon and saw down to the shoulder lines.

4 Cutting the shoulder lines. Set the board flat on a worktable and cut straight down along a shoulder line on the face to meet a tenon cut. Turn the board over and saw the second shoulder; then set the board on its edge and saw from the shoulder line to the tenon to remove the last piece of waste and to form the third shoulder.

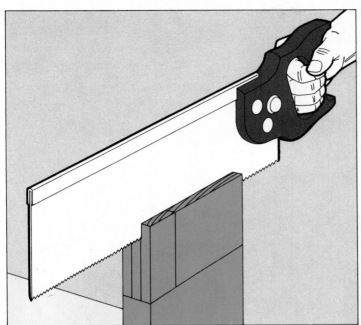

5 Finishing the corners. Grasp the blade of a chisel near the handle, place the flat side of the blade against the shoulder, and set the cutting edge in the corner where the shoulder and tenon meet. Raise one corner of the blade by tilting the handle away from you and slowly draw the chisel toward you to scrape any wood out of the shoulder-tenon corner.

Caution: This is one of the rare jobs in which you must chisel toward, rather than away from, your body; work slowly and take special care to keep your fingers out of the path of the blade.

The Ins and Outs of Rabbets and Dadoes

The traditional way to make a strong, gap-proof joint between boards—for attaching a fascia board, laying flooring, putting up paneling or finishing stairs—is with an interlocking dado or an overlapping rabbet. A rabbet is a step cut into the edge or end of a board. A dado is a channel cut within a board. Either cut can be made laboriously and slowly with a saw and chisel, quickly with a router, or very exactly with a radial arm saw.

To rabbet a board with a handsaw, make two cuts at right angles to each other along the edge; produce a dado by making several saw cuts spaced as close as possible to one another within the groove area, then chiseling out the wood. These hand methods, while adequate for a few cuts, are time-consuming and tend to be rough. For faster, more precise work, use a router—a power tool designed to cut dadoes and rabbets.

A router requires a guide to keep it cutting in a perfectly straight line. Some rabbeting bits have built-in ball-bearing guides. And special attachments that fasten to the tool base will guide the cutting of both rabbets and dadoes at the desired distance from the board edge. But you can make a simple guide yourself from scrap lumber and C clamps. If you want to cut identical rabbets or dadoes in a small number of boards, homemade jigs will guide the router on the boards. However, when construction calls for a variety of cuts in many pieces of lumber, the best tool is a radial arm saw equipped with either of two special attachments, a dado head or a wobbler *(page 99)*.

The Router's Speed: A Mixed Blessing

Routers spin their razor-sharp bits at 22,000 rpms or more—a speed that gives this power tool its advantages of precision and ease of use, but also makes the router dangerous.

Fast rotation creates a twisting force that gives the tool a tendency to pull away from its user and expose the sharp cutter. Even after the motor is turned off, the blade does not stop at once.

The high speed of the cutter also makes a router jump if you turn the motor on when the bit is in contact with wood; always keep the bit free when starting up. Handle the router firmly—never gingerly—and use both hands when cutting with it. This is especially important when making cuts—such as those with the grain or against the bit's natural tendency to move from left to right—that tend to cause "chatter," or vibration.

DEPTH SCALE

LOCKING SCREW

DEPTH MARK

Setting the depth of a cut. Set the router on the board, loosen the locking screw and turn the motor unit clockwise until the tip of the bit just touches the wood; set the depth scale to zero. Move the router bit to the edge of the board and lower the bit until the depth scale registers the desired depth; tighten the locking screw.

To adjust the bit in a router without a depth scale, mark the depth of the desired cut on the side of a board, then turn the motor unit or the depth-adjustment collar to lower the bit until it aligns with the depth mark *(inset)*.

Cut no deeper than ⅜ inch in one pass; lower the bit and make additional passes for deep cuts.

Guides for Straight Cuts

A self-guiding rabbet bit. This cutter has at its tip a ball-bearing pilot that rolls along the edge of the board and keeps the bit cutting at a uniform depth. To use the bit, hold the router with the bit overhanging the edge of the board 2 inches from the left end, turn the motor on and move the bit into the wood until the roller meets the board edge. Move the router from left to right, pressing the guide against the edge. Complete the rabbet by moving the router from right to left through the uncut edge. Each rabbet cutter is designed for one width of rabbet but depth is adjustable by the methods described at left, bottom.

A homemade guide for rabbets or dadoes. Clamp a perfectly straight piece of wood to the board to be cut and hold the router firmly against it as you feed the bit through the wood. To determine the position of the guide, first draw lines on the board for the width of the cut. Set the router on top of the board with the bit just above the surface; align the bit with the lines and mark the edge of the router base on the face of the board. Extend the mark across the board with a combination square and clamp the guide along this line.

To rout a board that is narrower than the router's base (*inset*), clamp a board of equal thickness beside the board to be cut; position a guide board atop this second board and nail through both into the worktable to secure them.

A commercial guide for rabbets or dadoes. This edge attachment fastens to the router base; mount it according to the manufacturer's instructions. To use it, measure from the edge of the proposed cut to the edge of the board and set the guide plate that distance from the corresponding edge of the bit; place the guide against the board edge and keep it in firm contact as you feed the bit through the wood.

To cut boards narrower than the router's base, clamp boards of equal thickness on each side of the piece to be cut (*inset*). Nail a stop board across the side boards at one end to steady the work. Clamp this assembly to the bench.

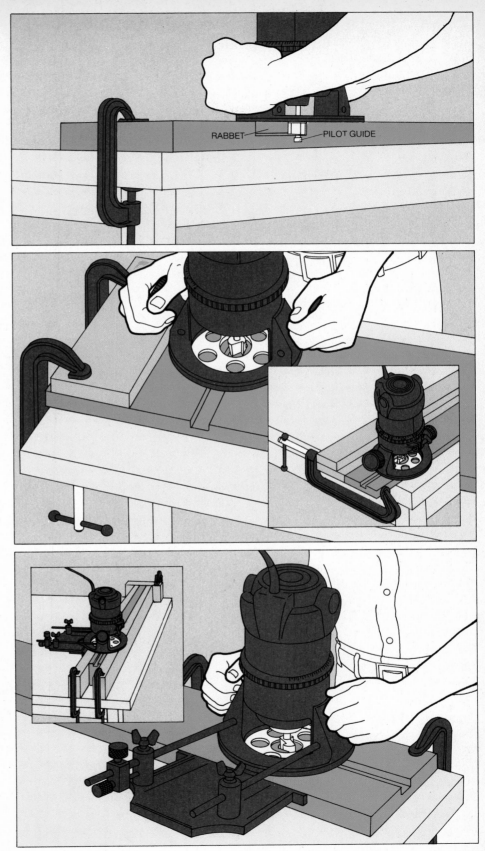

RABBET — PILOT GUIDE

Jigs for Speed and Control

A homemade jig. To cut many straight dadoes or rabbets in lumber of the same dimensions, lay two boards—each 4 inches wide, at least 2 feet long, and the same thickness as the lumber to be cut—parallel to each other; space them the width of the lumber to be cut. Screw two 1-by-2 crosspieces across the boards, spacing them the diameter of the router base; if a wide cut will require more than one pass with the router, add the difference between the width of the proposed cut and the diameter of the bit to the diameter of the base when calculating the spacing of the crosspieces.

Clamp the jig to a workbench, set the bit depth and make a notch the width of the desired cut on the inner edge of each 4-inch board, centering the notches between crosspieces.

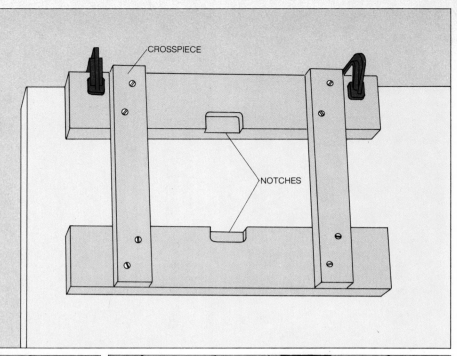

CROSSPIECE

NOTCHES

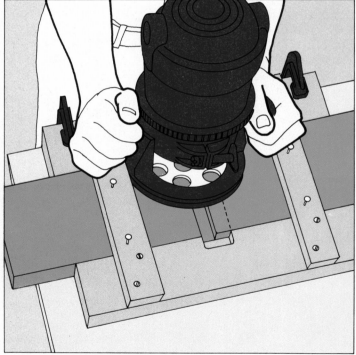

Making straight cuts. Measure and mark the dado or rabbet on each piece of lumber and slide the wood into the jig. Align the marks with the notch edges and nail through the crosspieces temporarily to secure the lumber. Set the router bit in one of the jig's notches, turn the motor on, and pass the tool steadily along one of the crosspieces to the other notch; for a wide cut like the one illustrated, make a second pass, guiding the router along the second crosspiece.

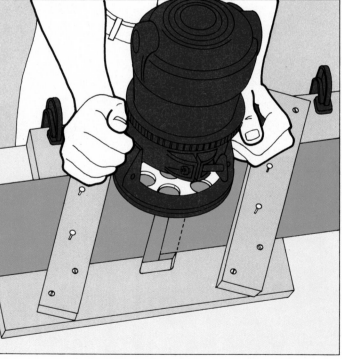

A jig for angles. To cut a dado at an angle or a rabbet on an angled end, alter the jig described at the top of this page by setting the crosspieces to the desired angle across the 4-inch boards and providing new or enlarged notches for the router bit. Cut the angles the same way as you cut straight dadoes and rabbets.

A jig for stopped cuts. To rout dadoes or rabbets that do not run completely across a board, alter the jig described opposite, top, by notching only one of the 4-inch boards and adding a 1-by-2 stop between the crosspieces. Screw the stop to the unnotched 4-inch board so that the distance from its edge to the inside edge of the desired cut equals the distance from the edge of the bit to the rim of the router base. Follow the technique used for straight cuts, turning the router off when its base hits the stop.

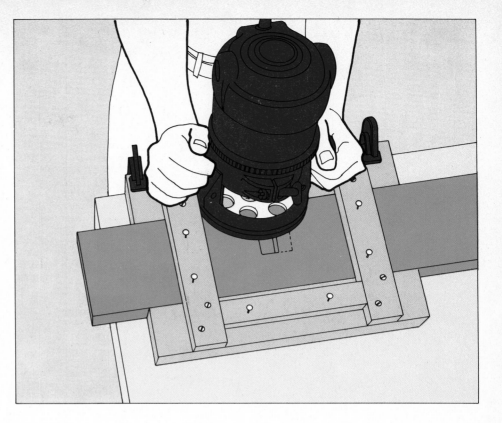

Dado Blades for a Radial Arm Saw

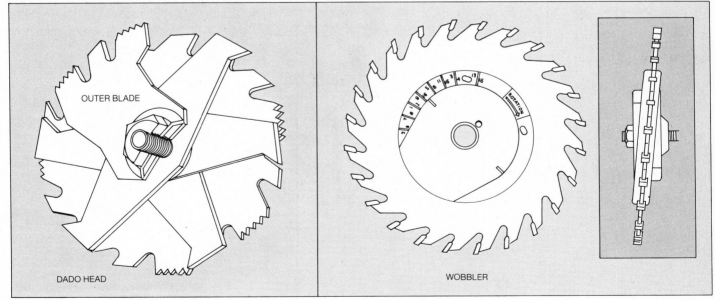

OUTER BLADE

DADO HEAD

WOBBLER

Two ways to cut a wide path. A radial arm saw can be adapted to cut dadoes and rabbets efficiently with either of two accessories. The dado head (left) replaces the regular blade with two saw blades separated by chippers and an assortment of washers. (In this drawing, the outer blade is largely cut away for clarity.) The width of cut—up to $13/16$ inch—is adjusted by assembling the blades with the appropriate chippers and washers. Less expensive, but also less precise, is the wobbler (right)—two wedge-shaped washers that grip the regular blade between them, angling it on the axle so that it chews out a wide path (inset). The wobbler washers are marked so that by turning them you can adjust for a cut as much as $13/16$ inch wide.

Routing a Custom Molding

Although lumberyards sell millwork—the moldings that trim doors, windows and mantels and form baseboards and chair rails—in many styles, you cannot always find the one you want. But with a router you can produce custom trims to suit your own taste.

Router bits for shaping decorative edges or grooves come in a large range of styles and sizes that can make cuts as much as 1⅝ inch wide and ¾ inch deep. By combining cuts with several bits, you can duplicate or create almost any molding. To check the cut that will be made by a bit or combination of bits, make test cuts on scrap wood. Use boards at least 1 inch thick, of white or ponderosa pine free of knots or warping.

A small amount of trim can be made by the normal routing technique, but if large amounts are called for—a roomful of window casings or baseboard, for example—convert your router into a home-made shaper (opposite) by mounting it on a simple wooden table, which enables you to repeat the same cut accurately in several pieces of wood. Mount the router upside down beneath the table, mount the table on a workbench or clamp it to sawhorses, then adjust the router-bit depth and the table fence for your cut.

Since the router's rotating bit is exposed above the table surface, be scrupulous about safety precautions. Keep hands well away from the moving bit and use push sticks to finish cuts. To make sure you can shut the tool off quickly and safely, power the router from a switched receptacle mounted on the worktable; connect the receptacle to your power source with 14-gauge flexible cord and a grounded plug.

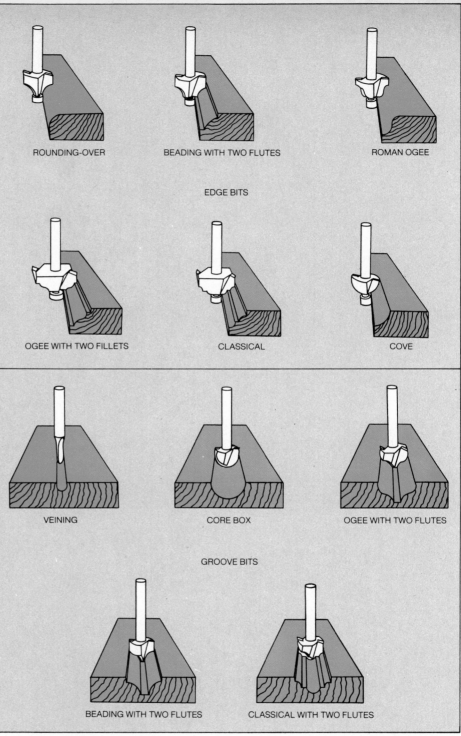

ROUNDING-OVER   BEADING WITH TWO FLUTES   ROMAN OGEE

EDGE BITS

OGEE WITH TWO FILLETS   CLASSICAL   COVE

VEINING   CORE BOX   OGEE WITH TWO FLUTES

GROOVE BITS

BEADING WITH TWO FLUTES   CLASSICAL WITH TWO FLUTES

A catalogue of special effects. This selection of router bits represents only a fraction of the profiles to choose from for forming edges and grooves. Edging bits generally have ball-bearing pilot guides that ride along the side of a board to help position the router. The width of any cut is limited by the width of the bit, but bits can be used in combination to create wider designs; for example, a deep cut with a core-box bit next to a shallow cut with a rounding-over bit would produce an ogee curve wider than the one that an ogee bit used alone can produce. The router's depth of cut is adjustable and some cutters, such as the ogee edging bit with two fillets, can produce more than one profile, depending on the depth to which the router is set.

A Router Table
for Mass Production

Building a router table. Fasten legs made of 2-by-8s on opposite sides of a piece of ½-inch plywood 2½ to 3 feet square with four countersunk wood screws. Locate the board's center by drawing diagonal lines from corner to corner and drill a hole ⅛ inch wider than the widest bit you are planning to use.

With the router's base removed, center the tool over the bit hole and mark the location of the screw holes in the base. Drill and countersink holes for the machine screws that will hold the router upside down under the table. For safety and convenience, plug the router cord into a switched receptacle mounted on the table.

Make a fence that is the same length as the table, using a perfectly straight piece of 1-by-2 lumber. In the center of one side of the fence, cut a semicircular notch to match the table's bit hole. Use C clamps to hold the fence to the table; you will then be able to move the fence to accommodate boards of any width.

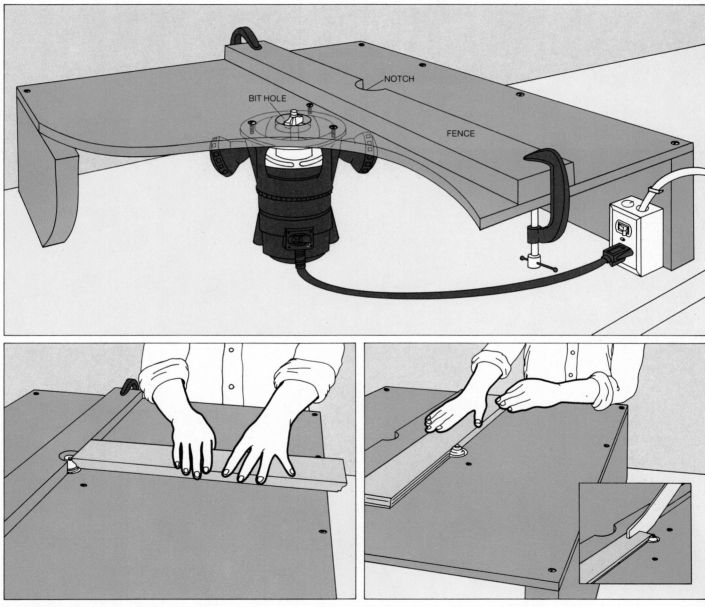

Shaping against the grain. Align the notched side of the fence over the bit hole and, with the bit rotating clockwise into the wood, push the lumber into and past the bit. Hold the wood firmly against both the table and the fence and keep your hands well away from the bit.

Shaping with the grain. Push the lumber between the router bit and the straight side of the fence, steadying the wood against the fence with one hand, feeding it past the cutter with the other. Finish the cut with a push stick to keep hands well away from the bit (*inset*).

Sharpening a Shaper to a Fine Cutting Edge

When a cutting tool that is used to remove thin parings of wood requires more than light pressure to do its job, its edge needs to be renewed; it should be sharpened by honing and stropping. If a cutting edge is nicked or the bevel leading to the edge has become thickened or rounded, the blade must be reshaped with a grinding wheel.

The shape of the cutting edge determines how it is honed. Tools with straight blades and edges, such as plane irons, wood chisels and some drawknives and hatchets, are honed by rubbing the beveled edge of the blade against whetstones—first medium-grit, then finer-grit—set on a flat surface. The burr, or wire edge, created by honing is removed by rubbing the flat side of the blade on a fine-grit whetstone.

Tools with edges that curve outward, such as adzes and some hatchets used for rough carpentry, are sharpened with a whetstone or round ax stone held in the hand. Tools with blades that are curved in cross section, such as gouges—curved chisels—and some drawknives, are trickier. The beveled outside curve of the blade is honed by rubbing it against a whetstone lying on a flat surface; the flat

inside curve is honed with a slipstone—a small, wedge-shaped stone having one rounded edge—held in the hand.

To accomplish these honing operations, a variety of whetstones are available. Natural stones made of the mineral novaculite—called Washita stones in medium grit, Arkansas stones in fine grit—cut slowly but produce an extremely keen edge that stays sharp longer than one honed on an artificial stone. Considerably less expensive than natural stones, artificial stones are made of either aluminum oxide (sold under such trade names as India and Alundum) or silicon carbide (sold as Carborundum or Crystolon). Silicon carbide cuts faster, aluminum oxide gives a sharper edge. Most versatile are combination man-made stones, medium grit on one side, fine on the other.

Soak new stones overnight in mineral oil or a lightweight machine oil. Before each use, apply a light coating of oil; after use, wipe the stone with a clean cloth. Store stones in containers—covered wooden boxes are common—to keep them clean and safe from breakage.

To complete a sharpening operation, strop a blade on a piece of smooth leather that has been rubbed with a little oil,

jeweler's rouge or emery powder. Tools can also be stropped with a buffing wheel mounted on a grinder. Honed tools should slice cleanly through paper or shave the hair on your arm.

If a tool requires more than sharpening and must be reshaped to eliminate nicks and correct the bevel, use a grinder, generally with a medium-fine 60-grit or 100-grit vitrified aluminum oxide wheel. Follow the manufacturer's recommendations for the operation of your grinder and observe the safety precautions for grinders (box, page 77)—because of their high speed of rotation, they can throw off fragments with killing force. Cut metal from the edge, working slowly, and dip the tool in water frequently to cool it. Overheating the metal will draw its temper, so that it will not take a sharp edge.

Careful storage can minimize the kinds of damage that lead to regrinding. Hang tools in racks, sheathe them in leather or keep them in canvas rolls. Oil each edge lightly after each use to inhibit rust. Store a plane on its side, with the iron retracted so that it does not protrude through the sole plate; store cutters or blades for power tools in the protective cases in which they are packaged.

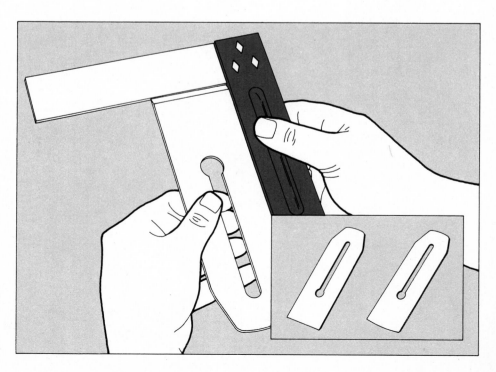

Straight-edged shapers. Use a try square to check the edge of any wood chisel or the iron of a block plane designed for precise cuts; the edges should be perfectly straight and should have perfectly square corners. The corners of a plane iron designed for general-purpose work should be slightly rounded (inset, left). The iron of a jack or jointer plane, designed for the fast removal of larger amounts of wood, is ground with a slightly convex edge (inset, right), the center about $\frac{1}{32}$ inch higher than the corners.

Curved shapers. Trace the curved silhouette of a hatchet or adz and use the tracing as a template when reshaping damaged edges. The cutting edge of a firmer gouge, like that of a chisel or a plane iron, is perpendicular to the tool's blade; the blade itself is curved and is beveled on the outside of the curve *(inset)*.

Bevel angles. Use a protractor bevel, which combines the features of a protractor and a T bevel, to measure the angle of a tool's beveled edge when grinding the tool. The bevels of chisels, gouges, plane irons and drawknives are hollowed slightly by a grinding wheel *(inset);* the bevels should be twice as long as the thickness of the blades and should be cut at a 25° angle to the flat side of the blade. (Chisels used for precision cuts or easier-to-cut woods are sometimes ground to a 15° or 20° angle, but these thin edges are especially susceptible to nicking.) Hatchets are ground with slightly convex bevels for greater strength. Some have only one bevel, ground at a 25° angle; others are double-beveled, with the two bevels at a 30° angle.

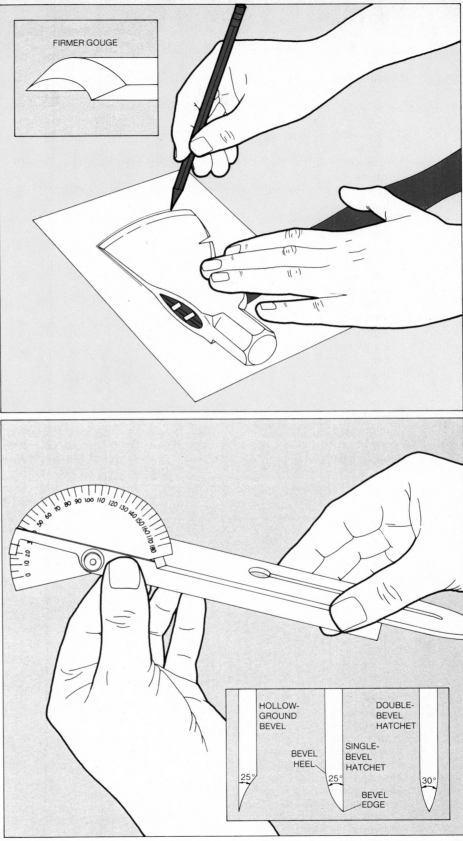

FIRMER GOUGE

HOLLOW-GROUND BEVEL

BEVEL HEEL

DOUBLE-BEVEL HATCHET

SINGLE-BEVEL HATCHET

BEVEL EDGE

25°

25°

30°

Honing a Straight Edge

1 Positioning the bevel. Standing with your feet slightly apart, grip the tool comfortably and lay its bevel flat against a medium-grit whetstone; hold the bevel lightly against the whetstone with the fingers of your free hand. Brace your lower forearm firmly against your body and stiffen the wrist of the hand holding the tool to maintain the angle of the bevel as it rests on the stone.

If you find it hard to brace the tool on the stone, use a honing jig *(inset)* to hold chisels or plane irons at the correct angle.

2 Sharpening the bevel. Rock your body in small circles from the ankles, so that the bevel moves in small circles or ellipses; with a honing jig, make straight push-pull strokes. Exert pressure on the circular or straight pulling strokes; use the pushing strokes to reposition the bevel for the next stroke. Keep the bevel flat on the stone—rocking it will dull the edge or round the bevel.

When you have worn a uniform, dull-gray scratch pattern across the bevel and no shiny spots show along the edge, repeat Steps 1 and 2 on a fine whetstone until you can feel a burr, or wire edge *(inset)*, when you run a finger up the flat side of the blade and past the edge.

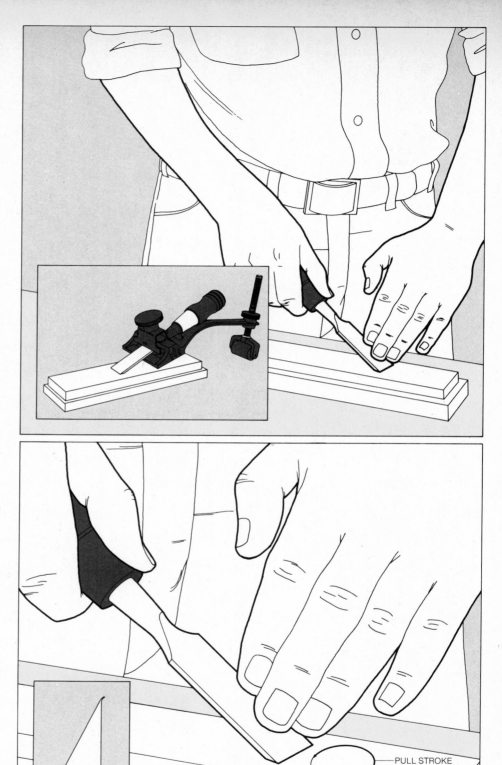

PULL STROKE

PUSH STROKE

3 Removing the wire edge. Turn the blade over, hold it flat against a fine whetstone and pull the blade repeatedly along the length of the stone until you can no longer feel the wire edge. Finish honing with pulling strokes on a leather strop, on both the flat and beveled sides of the blade.

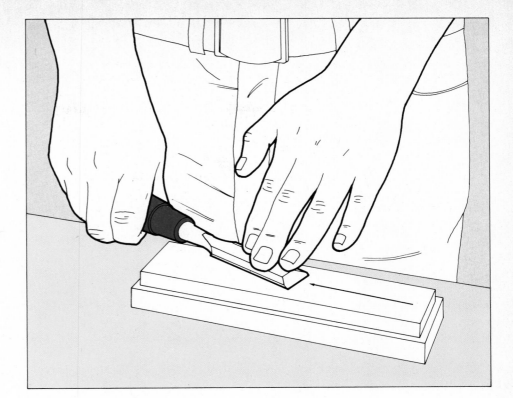

Honing and Stoning a Curved Edge

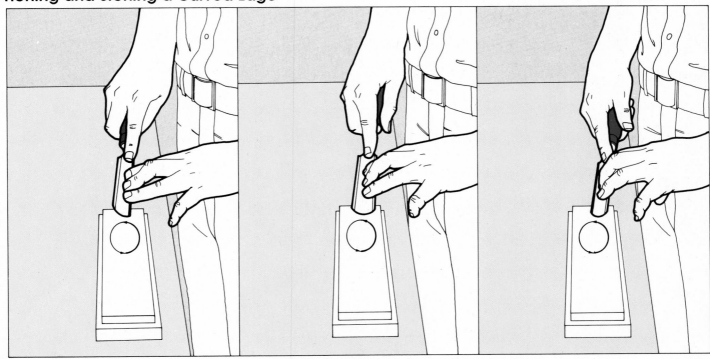

1 Honing a firmer gouge. Hold the tool as shown in Step 1 (*opposite*) and sharpen it as described in Step 2 (*opposite*), but roll the tool from side to side as you work. Start on one side of the curved edge (*left*), and move the bevel in several circles; roll the tool slightly, and hone the middle of the bevel (*center*), then roll it again to hone the opposite side (*right*). Repeat rolling and honing until the entire surface of the bevel has a uniform scratch pattern.

2 **Removing the wire edge from a curve.** Hold the curved edge of a slipstone flat against the inside of a firmer-gouge blade and slide the stone back and forth; repeat the strokes along the entire edge, always keeping the slipstone flat against the blade. Strop the outer curve on a length of leather lying on a flat surface; strop the inner curve with a piece of folded leather.

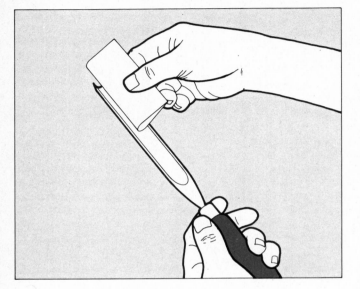

Sharpening a Convex Bevel

Honing a hatchet. Hold a coarse or medium whetstone against the very edge of the hatchet's convex bevel; do not hold the stone flat against the bevel or you will deform the bevel shape. Move the stone along the edge in small circles, then repeat the process with a finer stone. On a double-beveled blade, honing both bevels will remove the wire edge. If the blade has a single bevel, remove the wire edge from the flat side with a whetstone (*page 105, Step 3*).

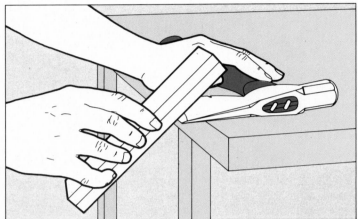

Restoring a Hollow Bevel with a Grinding Wheel

1 **Setting the tool rest.** Loosen the wing nut of the tool rest and adjust the rest so that, with the tool flat against it, the tool bevel meets the face of the grinding wheel at the correct angle and at a point above the wheel axis.

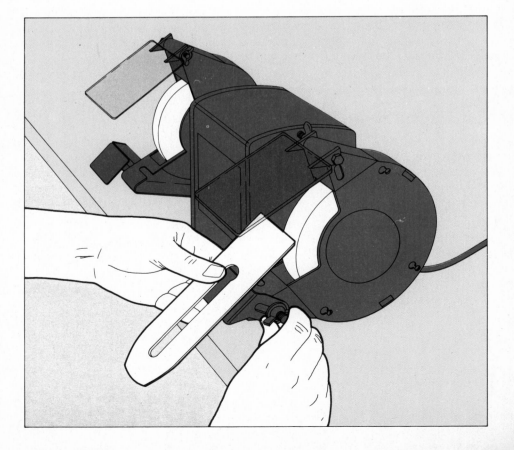

2 **Grinding the bevel.** With the grinder on, bring the edge of the tool into light contact with the circumference of the wheel. If you are grinding a straight-edged tool, move it back and forth across the circumference; if you are grinding a firmer gouge, roll it to present all parts of the bevel to the wheel. Make light cuts and quench the blade frequently in water. Use a protractor bevel repeatedly to check the angle as you grind it. When the bevel is held to strong light, you should see a uniformly shiny scratch pattern; a patchy surface with both shiny and dull spots indicates an unevenly ground bevel.

Restoring a Convex Bevel

Freehand grinding. Hold the heel of a convex bevel against the grinding wheel and pass the blade across the circumference; if the tool has a curved edge, like the one at right, move it in a small arc to keep the heel of the bevel against the wheel. Before making the next pass across the wheel, raise the heel slightly and rock the edge forward; repeat this procedure until the edge of the bevel passes across the wheel. Cool the blade frequently, check the angle with a protractor bevel, and check the outline of a curved edge against your tracing of it *(page 103, top)*.

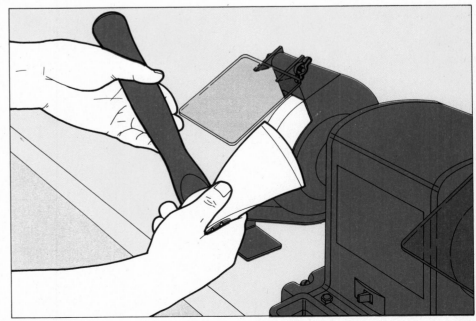

A joint for a window sash. The slot and the projection, factory-cut in these two boards, lock together in a secure mortise-and-tenon joint. Years of rough use may loosen such a joint. If this happens, the joint can be separated and the parts coated with glue, tapped back together with a wooden mallet—itself an example of precise joinery—then pressed with a steel clamp until the glue sets and takes tight hold.

Until the last century, houses were put together by the ancient art of joinery. One end or edge of a piece of wood was shaped to fit into a mating shape in the end of another piece. The two pieces interlocked like the parts of a jigsaw puzzle, and the stresses of weight, wind and movement, which act to pull apart the elements of a house, were resisted by the shapes of the wood. There were no nails; they were too costly to use for the routine purpose of fastening together parts of a house.

The machine age changed this way of building; metal, not sculpted ends, began to hold together most of the wood in a house. Steel, once costly, became plentiful and cheap. Nails no longer had to be forged and cut by hand but could be mass-produced by the machines that spun out threads of steel and readily chopped them to any length. Over the decades, a bewildering array of metal fasteners has been developed to make flat-faced connections strong and neat, thus saving the time and painstaking labor of sculpting wood ends and edges into interlocking shapes.

There are screws for joints that have to be extra strong, bolts for fastening timbers, corrugated or toothed fasteners to hold delicate pieces of wood, and splines for stair rails. For heavier joints, metal is shaped into framing anchors that strap joists and rafters into place. There are even special nails that are made to hold extra tight—some of these are coated with resin that heats as the nail is driven into the wood to form an adhesive bond with the wood, while others have spiral shanks to increase their surface area and create more friction with the wood.

Yet for all the versatility of metal fasteners, some wood-shaped joints have survived—and are used today for the same reason that they were developed hundreds of years ago: they hold better. Their extra grip is needed where a small, weak joint, if rigidly connected, might work loose under repeatedly varying loads of changing stresses. Most are factory-made, in parts bought assembled from a mill, and demand attention only if they need to be reglued or, in rare instances, repaired with a hand-cut replacement part.

The top of a door jamb, for example, is stepped into the side jambs in a rabbet joint, to help resist the twisting force of door slams. In window sashes and doors, mortise-and-tenon joints (*opposite*) hold against repeated pushes and pulls. Stair treads and risers are made with grooved joints to counter the shifting weight of the people using them. In these and several other joints around the house, metal fasteners must take a secondary role: the skills of the old carpenters, the beauty of shaped wood, and the strength of wood bearing on wood have survived the advances of the machine age.

An Arsenal of Specialized Metal Fasteners

Most joints in wood rely on metal fasteners. Although some joints are held by glue and others are shaped in interlocking parts, nails, screws, bolts and a host of specialized steel connectors give woodworkers the fastest, most efficient means of joinery. So many of these fasteners have been devised that choosing the correct one for a specific job can be difficult. The decision must take into account the strength needed for the joint, the possibility that it may have to be unfastened at a later time and the importance of its appearance. For the conventional solution to most problems in joining rough or finish pieces of wood, refer to the chart on pages 112-113.

Nails, the most common fasteners, are quick, easy and inexpensive. Like all metal fasteners, they work by friction: a driven nail displaces wood fibers, which clamp the shank in place. However, nails with long, sharp points, though they enter wood easily, may split the fibers apart.

Blunt-pointed nails, either factory-made or blunted on the job, hold better because the blunt point clears a path through the wood and leaves a tight sleeve of unsplit fibers around the shank.

Once a nail is in place, two kinds of force can dislodge it. One kind, shearing stress, is exerted at an angle perpendicular to the shank. The other, withdrawal stress, is applied parallel and opposite to the direction of entry. A nail withstands shearing better than withdrawal stress, and should be driven across the grain, so that the main force against it, once it is in place, is shearing force.

Screws have greater holding power than nails do against withdrawal stress because their threads present a larger surface area, creating greater friction with the wood fibers. What is more, they are easy to remove without splintering or gouging wood. But they are more expensive than nails and take more time to install. Before you can screw two pieces

of wood together, you must drill one or more pilot holes (*page 119, text*).

Nuts and bolts are less commonly used than nails and screws, because both ends of the bolt must be accessible, an impossibility in many situations. However, they do form exceptionally tight, strong joints between pieces that are too large for the common fasteners. Still other fasteners are relatively specialized. For finish work, splines, which are thin metal plates, and corrugated or toothed fasteners make tight joints where nails or screws would split the wood, as in counter tops or frames for window screens. In rough construction, shaped metal plates called anchors or framing connectors secure structural members.

Glues, though more common in cabinetmaking than in house carpentry, add to the strength of any metal fastener. Epoxy resin, casein glue, vegetable glue and synthetic resin glue are all commonly used in joining wood.

From Common Nails to Nuts and Bolts

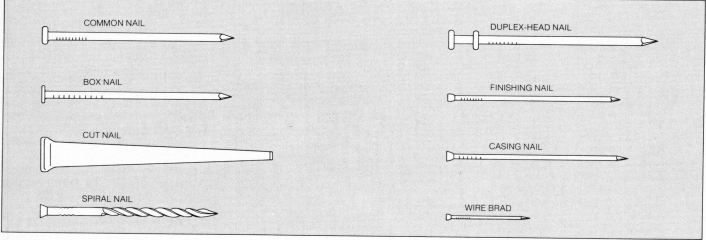

Nails. Common nails are used in general construction; box nails, almost identical, have a thinner shaft and are used on thin boards where splitting is a danger. Common nails and box nails are used for jobs in which the appearance of the surface is not important. Both types are available with a resin coating, which heats as the nail is driven and forms an adhesive bond between the nail and the wood.

Cut nails have two main uses: to join wood to masonry, and to give a rustic appearance when exposed in wood flooring. In tongue-and-

groove flooring joints, spiral nails are hdden from view but tightly grip the subfloor and the joists below. Duplex-head nails are designed for temporary installations, such as scaffolding and bracing—the top heads, raised above the wood, are easy to grip when the nails are removed. Finishing nails and casing nails, used in finish work, are almost interchangeable, though the casing nail has a slightly thicker shank and provides greater strength for heavier jobs. Both have small heads, which can easily be driven below the surface of the wood with a nail set. The wire brad, smallest nail of all, looks like a fin-

ishing nail but has a different system of sizes; it fastens the thinnest pieces of wood.

Nail sizes are usually given in "penny" ratings, which are not easily translated into lengths because the ratings arose from the nails' prices per pound in old England. The smallest nails designated in this way are twopenny—1 inch long. The largest are 60-penny—6 inches long—although nails longer than 20-penny generally are sized in inches. Today many boxes of nails specify length in inches. Nails shorter than twopenny are designated in fractions of an inch.

Screws. Screws for woodworking all have sharp threads that taper to a point. They differ in size, head shape and slotting, and some no longer have the traditional smooth shank.

Lag bolts, or lag screws, are the largest screws and are used for heavy work. Their square or hexagonal heads are turned by wrenches; some have slots and can be turned by screwdrivers as well. Lag bolts are sized in inches for both length and diameter.

Standard wood screws—those with smooth shanks and slotted heads—are available in three head shapes and two slot types. Flat-heads are the most common because they are easily countersunk below the wood surface and covered with putty. Oval-heads and round-heads generally are left exposed for decorative effect. Both single and Phillips slots are equally common; you need a special screwdriver for Phillips screws, but you have better control of the screwhead. Standard screws are sized by diameter in gauge numbers and by length in inches—standard gauges are No. 4 (⅛-inch diameter) through No. 14 (¼-inch diameter).

Sheet-metal screws, which have threads extending to the heads, also are used in woodworking, especially for attaching plywood panels and hardware. They come in the three common head shapes plus a fourth called a pan-head, and have either Phillips or standard slots. They are sized like standard wood screws.

Bolts. Though most common in metalwork, bolts, washers and nuts have important uses in wood construction. Rail bolts, the most specialized, join the rails of a stairway to newel posts and goosenecks. Stove bolts are used to join 2-by-4s for rough shelving; machine and carriage bolts, stronger and heavier, are used in steel-reinforced headers.

Bolts are sized by diameter of the thread and by length from the bottom of the head to the end of the bolt. Flat-head stove bolts, however, are measured from the top of the head.

Finishing fasteners. Special fasteners with corrugated edges or projecting teeth reinforce weak nail joints between butted pieces, such as counter tops or the mitered corners of window-screen frames. Splines, which are thinner than the others and less obtrusive, are used on thick pieces in situations where nails or screws would be ugly and insecure—typically to join two sections of stair rail, end to end.

Anchors. Framing anchors come in many shapes, designed for a wide variety of connections. Originally developed in the 1940s to strengthen joints of buildings located in hurricane areas, they are increasingly popular because they eliminate toenailing and difficult hammering angles. An anchor is fastened to wood by eightpenny common nails or by shorter nails packaged with the anchor by the manufacturer.

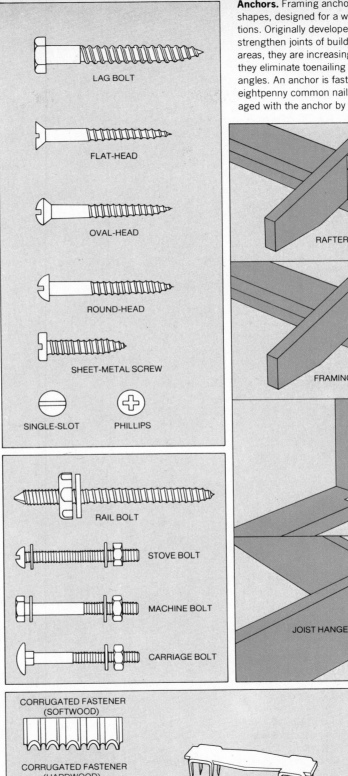

LAG BOLT

FLAT-HEAD

OVAL-HEAD

ROUND-HEAD

SHEET-METAL SCREW

SINGLE-SLOT   PHILLIPS

RAIL BOLT

STOVE BOLT

MACHINE BOLT

CARRIAGE BOLT

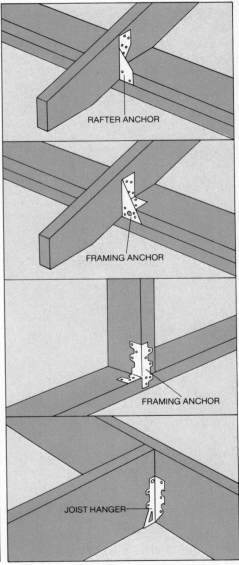

RAFTER ANCHOR

FRAMING ANCHOR

FRAMING ANCHOR

JOIST HANGER

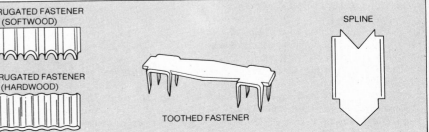

CORRUGATED FASTENER (SOFTWOOD)

CORRUGATED FASTENER (HARDWOOD)

TOOTHED FASTENER

SPLINE

A Fastener for Every Job

Job	Fastener	Size	Placement	Comments
Baseboard	Finishing nail	8d(2½″)	2 at each corner, 2 at each stud	Drive 1 nail horizontally through the middle of the board, the other downward at a 45° angle into the sole plate.
Base shoe	Finishing nail	4d(1½″)	16″ apart	Drive nail downward at a 45° angle just above middle of shoe.
Bridging between joists				
Diagonal	Box nail	8d(2½″)	2 at each end	Nail through bridging into joists.
Solid	Box nail	16d(3½″)	2 at each end	Face-nail through joists into staggered bridging.
Cabinet to wall	Flat-head screw	No. 8 × 2¾″	At studs	
Carriage, stair				
To header	Common nail	16d(3½″)	6 evenly spaced	Use framing anchor where possible.
To wall	Common nail	16d(3½″)	2 at each stud	
Casing, door and window	Finishing nail	4d(1½″) 6d(2″)	About 12″ apart	Drive 4d nails on inside edge, 6d nails on outside edge.
Ceiling molding	Finishing nail	8d(2½″)	1 at each corner, 1 at each stud	
Chair rail	Finishing nail	6d(2″)	2 at each stud	Nail through grooves if possible.
Collar beam to rafter:				
1-by lumber	Common nail	8d(2½″)	4 at each end	Drive 2 nails into beam, 2 into rafter.
2-by lumber	Common nail	10d(3¼″)		
Counter tops				
Section to section	Corrugated fastener		1½″ apart	
To cabinet base	Flat-head screw	No. 10	1 at each corner	Choose screw length so that it will not penetrate counter-top surface.
Deck, outdoor	Common nail	16d(3½″)	2 at each joist	Use galvanized nails only.
Door stop	Finishing nail	4d(1½″)	8″ to 10″ apart	
Fascia board	Box nail	6d(2″) or 8d(2½″)	2 at each rafter	
Firestop	Box nail	16d(3½″)	2 at each end	
Flooring				
25/32″ thick	Spiral or cut nail	7d(2¼″) or 8d(2½″)	10″ to 12″ apart	Angle spiral nails 45° at base of tongue; face-nail cut nails and leave exposed for rustic look.
½″ thick	Spiral or cut nail	5d(1¾″) or 6d(2″)	8″ to 10″ apart	
Girder, built-up	Common nail	20d(4″)	Staggered every 24″	Nail from both sides.
Header				
Wooden	Common nail	16d(3½″)	Staggered 12″ apart	Drive nails 4″ from each end and ¾″ from each edge.
Steel reinforced	Carriage bolt	½″ × 4½″	Staggered 16″ apart	Fasten 2 bolts at each end, 4″ from edge, 6″ from end.
Joist				
Overlap at partition or girder	Common nail	16d(3½″)	2 on each side	Face-nail at slight angle.

Job	Fastener	Size	Placement	Comments
Plate				
Partition top plate, across joists	Common nail	10d(3")	2 at each joist	
Partition top plate, parallel to joists	Common nail	16d(3½")	24" apart	Nail to joist or blocking.
Partition sole plate to floor	Common nail	10d(3")	12" apart	
Bearing wall sole plate, to joist	Common nail	16d(3½")	16" apart	
Doubled top plate	Common nail	16d(3½")	16" apart	Lap joints of lower plate 4 feet on both sides.
Rafter				
To ridge beam	Common nail	16d(3½") and 8d(2½")	3 on each side of beam	Face-nail with 16d nails, toenail with 8d.
To top plate	Common nail	8d(2½")	1 on each side	Toenail or use framing anchor.
Hip or valley rafter, to common rafter	Common nail	10d(3")	2 on one side, 1 on the other	Toenail.
Jack rafter, to hip rafter	Common nail	10d(3")	2 on one side, 1 on the other	Toenail.
Riser, stair	Finishing nail	6d(2")	3 at each carriage	Drill pilot holes in hardwood.
Sheathing				
Roof or wall, 5/16" or ⅜" plywood	Common nail	6d(2")	6" apart on edges; 12" apart on intermediate studs or rafters	
Roof or wall, ½" plywood	Common nail	8d(2½")		
Roof, board	Common nail	8d(2½")	2 at each rafter	
Studs				
To top plate	Common nail	16d(3½")	2 at each end	
To sole plate	Common nail	8d(2½")	2 on one side, 1 on the other	Toenail or use framing anchor.
Cripple studs to headers and sills	Common nail	16d(3½") or 8d(2½")	2 at ends or 2 on one side, 1 on the other	Face-nail (16d) or toenail (8d) as required.
Jack to king stud	Common nail	16d(3½")	6 nails evenly spaced and staggered	Face-nail at slight angle.
King stud to header	Common nail	16d(3½")	4 at each end	
To adjoining wall	Common nail	16d(3½")	16" apart	
Subflooring				
½" plywood	Common nail	6d(2")	6" apart on edges, 10" apart on intermediate joists	
⅝" or ¾" plywood	Common nail	8d(2½")	6" apart on edges, 10" apart on intermediate joists	
Tread, stair	Finishing nail	8d(2½")	3 at each carriage	Drill pilot holes in hardwood.
Underlayment to subflooring				
⅜" or ½" plywood	Common nail	4d(1½")	6" apart on edges, 8" apart inside	
⅜" particleboard	Common nail	4d(1½")	6" apart on edges, 10" apart inside	

Matching the fastener to the job. In the first column of this chart, common fastening jobs in house carpentry are listed alphabetically. The second column gives the recommended fastener for each job; the third, the recommended size for the fastener. Nail sizes are given in two ways: the traditional "penny" notation is written as a numeral and *d* (the old British abbreviation for *penny*); next, in parentheses, is the length in inches. In screw sizes, the first figure is the gauge number, the second is the length; in carriage-, rail- and lag-bolt sizes, the first figure is the bolt diameter, the second is the length. The fourth column indicates the usual placement of the fasteners, and the fifth contains special comments. Unless otherwise indicated, nails should be face-nailed—that is, driven straight through the face of one piece and into another piece.

How a Pro Hammers a Nail

The first hard lesson every amateur carpenter learns is the difficulty of driving a nail straight and true. The skill of the professional comes only with practice, but some basic facts make expertise easier to acquire. You need to know how to choose a hammer, how to set the nail at the proper angle and how to adjust your swing to the location of the nail. Even pulling nails involves special techniques.

Good nailing begins with the right hammer. The ones most used for carpentry come with several types of heads and handles and in several weights. A lightweight 7- or 13-ounce hammer is best for finish work; it drives finishing nails easily and is less likely to mar trim if its face hits the wood. A heavier 16-ounce hammer can be used for finish as well as framing work, and is the preferred weight for general use; the other common size, 20-ounce, is used solely on framing jobs.

Handles are available in wood, steel and fiberglass, but choosing among them depends less on a specific job than on feel and ease of maintenance. Wooden handles absorb more of the shock of hammering, but they eventually loosen and must be retightened (below). Steel and fiberglass handles rarely come loose, but both vibrate badly when driving large nails; of the two, fiberglass is lighter but occasionally breaks, while steel is virtually indestructible.

The major difference in hammer heads concerns the shape of the claw, which may be curved or straight. The curved type, more common in house carpentry, is better for pulling nails because its head can roll back farther with a nail in its grip. The straight-claw hammer is used mainly for framing and renovation work; its claw more easily wedges between boards to pry them apart. Some straight-claw hammers—and a few curved-claw models—have a cross-checked face that reduces the tendency of the face to slip off a nail but leaves a checked pattern on the wood surface.

Nailing technique varies, not with the type of hammer but with the way the nail is to be driven—into a board face, at an angle for toenailing, or straight through and bent-over for clinch-nailing. If you do bend a nail or drive it wrong, do not waste time trying to straighten it—simply pull it out and drive a new one. The claws of a hammer generally will do the pulling job well enough; such specialized tools as a cat's paw and a nail puller (page 118) make the job faster and easier.

Never forget that hammering is hard on muscles and bones. Carpenters fall prey to the same ailments that affect tennis players. If, in the course of a job, you feel twinges of pain in an arm or shoulder, stop immediately and rest.

Tightening a wooden handle. Use a cold chisel to make a groove $\frac{1}{16}$ inch deep in the top of the handle, halfway between and parallel with the fastening wedges already inserted in the handle top at the factory. Set a new wedge, sold at hardware stores, into the groove and drive it into the handle with a ball-peen hammer until the wedge barely moves with each blow; if you drive it further you may split the handle. Using a hacksaw, cut all the protruding portion of the wedge flush with the top of the hammer head.

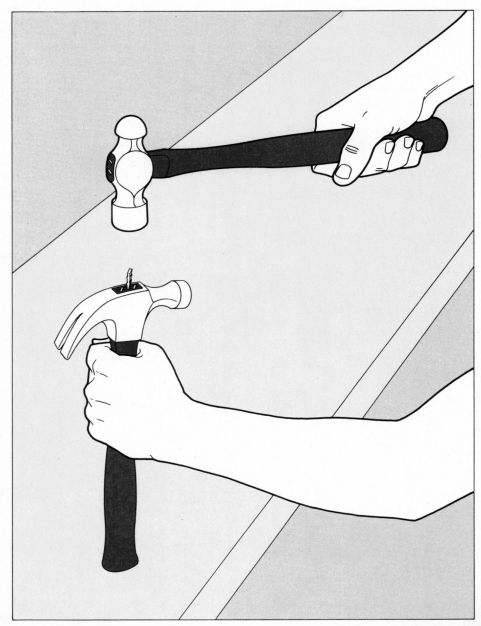

Starting the nail. Hold the nail near its tip between your thumb and index finger, angle it about 10° from you—it will straighten under the hammer blows—and tap it lightly. Support the nail with your fingers until it is driven deep enough into the wood to stand by itself.

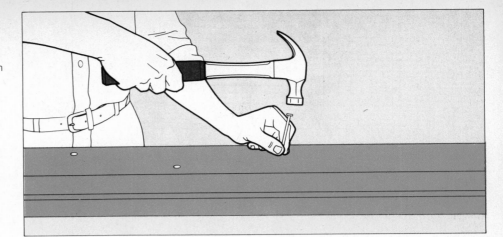

Driving the nail home. Swing the hammer up to a point just behind your ear; then deliver the blow so that when the hammer strikes the nail its handle is at a 90° angle with the nail shaft, and the nailhead is directly below the center of its face. Adjust the force of the last blow to drive the head of the nail flush with the wood surface.

Nailing out. When you must nail a joint located between knee and shoulder height in a space too restricted for a normal swing, nail horizontally in front of your body, using a stroke called nailing out. Grip the hammer with your thumb on the back of the handle for better control. Hold the hammer with its head in front of you, bend your arm back toward your body and drive the nail by swinging your arm outward.

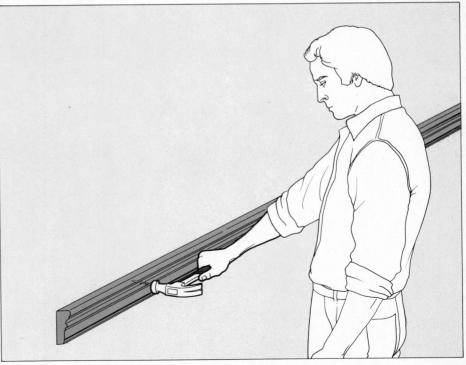

Nailing up. When the joint you are nailing is above your head, grip the hammer as you would for nailing out *(page 115, bottom)* and swing your arm upward with a full wrist, elbow and shoulder motion. If the work is so high that your arm would be almost fully extended at the end of the swing and the hammer cannot hit the nail squarely, stand on a ladder so that your striking position resembles that shown at right.

Toenailing. To brace the board being toenailed (in this example, a stud being fastened to a sole plate), drive a nail at a 70° angle partway into the joint between two pieces; to make a check in the accuracy of the final toenails, draw a short straight line along the middle of the piece being toenailed and onto the second piece. Locate the starting point of the first toenail so that one third of the nail, if driven at a 45° angle, will lie in the piece being toenailed and two thirds in the second piece; for an eightpenny nail driven into 2-by-4s, this point is about 1 inch from the end of the piece being toenailed. Start the nail at a 90° angle *(right, top)*; when you have driven it about ½ inch into the wood, tip it up about 45° and drive at that angle *(right, bottom)* until its head dents the wood. If a second nail is needed, drive it in the same way.

Remove the bracing nail and toenail the pieces together on the other side. Check the pencil line; if its two parts have been displaced, hammer one side of the toenailed piece to bring the lines together. In rough framing an error of ¼ inch is generally acceptable.

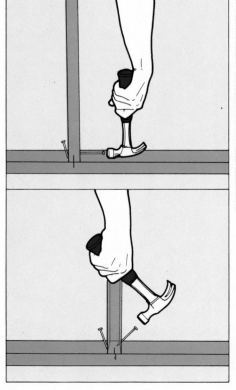

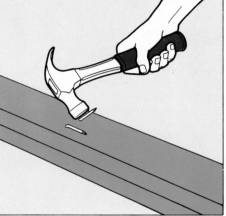

Clinch-nailing. To make a composite header or support post by doubling boards, place the boards face to face and drive through them nails 30 per cent longer than their combined thickness. Drive the nailheads flush, turn the pieces over, set them on a hard, flat surface and hammer the projecting nail shanks at an angle, bending them as close to the surface as possible. Align the shanks with the grain for a smoother surface, but across the grain for a stronger joint. When the shanks are nearly horizontal, strike them with two or three vertical blows to seat them deeply in the wood.

Driving and Setting a Finishing Nail

1 Starting the nail. Hold the nail as you would for rough work (*page 115, top*), but wrap your fingers around the hammer handle and set your thumb along the handle as illustrated. Hit the nail lightly, supporting it with your fingers until it can stand by itself, then driving it until its head is about 1/8 inch above the surface of the wood.

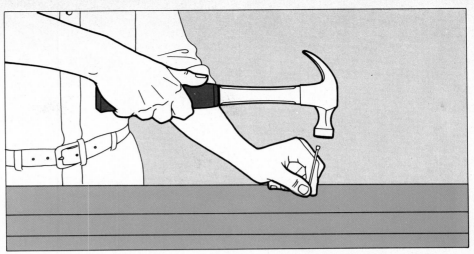

2 Setting the nail. Hold a nail set near its tip between thumb and index finger and center the recessed tip over the head of the nail. Rest your little finger on the wood to steady your hand, then hit the top of the set solidly with the hammer to drive the head of the nail about $1/16$ inch below the surface of the wood.

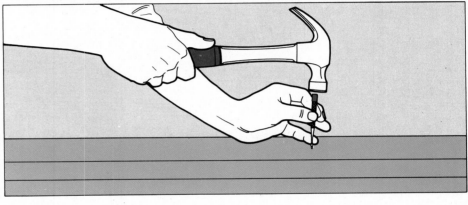

Three Ways to Pull a Nail

Starting with a curved-claw hammer. If the head of the nail is above the surface of the wood, slip the claw of the hammer around it; if the head is below the surface, set the end of the claw on the wood just next to it and strike the face of the hammer with a mallet until the claw engages the nailhead. Pull the handle of the hammer to a nearly vertical position and disengage the claw from the nailhead.

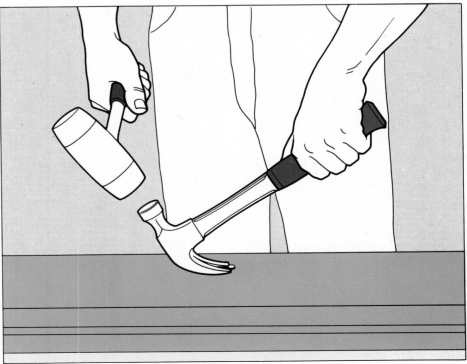

Freeing a nail with a curved claw. Place a piece of scrap—about as thick as the height of the half-pulled nail above the surface—next to the nail and set the head of the hammer on the scrap. Slip the claw around the nailhead and pull the nail out of the board.

Using a cat's paw. The claw of this prybar/nail puller is set around the head of the nail—if the head is below the surface of the wood, strike the curved section at the back of the tool with a rubber-faced mallet to drive the claw under the head. Then pull back on the handle to remove the nail. When you need to pull a nail from finish trim, set a thin piece of scrap under the heel of the cat's paw to protect the wood.

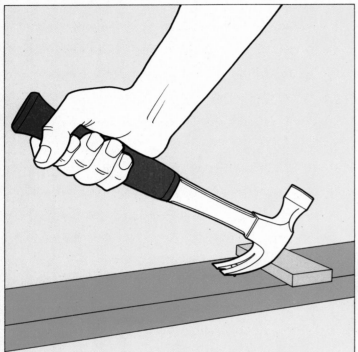

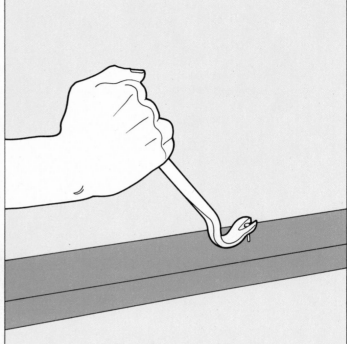

Using a nail puller. This special tool pulls nails quickly and easily. Position the pincers above the nailhead, opening them so they are slightly wider than the nailhead (*right*). Hold the handle attached to the pincers, then raise the sliding iron handle and slam it down repeatedly to sink the pincers beneath the nailhead. Close the pincers around the head.

Tilt the pincers sideways (*far right*), using the short handle attached to the pincers as a lever. Slowly pull the nail.

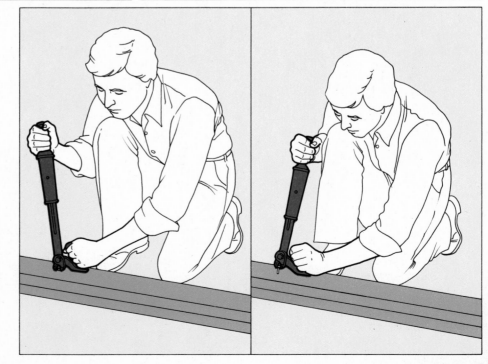

The Extra Strength of a Wood Screw

As fasteners of wood, screws have several advantages over nails. They bind pieces tighter, they do not mar the surface either entering or exiting, and with the proper pilot holes they do not split wood. But since they take more time and trouble to use than nails, they are reserved for joints that need extra strength or precision assembly or that may have to be dismantled.

The fuss involved in installing screws is minimized by using the right tools—properly maintained—not only to drive the screws but to drill the holes they require. All screws need at least one hole and some need as many as three. A pilot hole is the only hole required for those screws that are threaded all the way to the head, like sheet-metal screws or the screws often supplied with hardware kits or used for plywood.

Other screws require additional holes. Standard wood screws and lag bolts have smooth shanks between their threads and their heads; to accommodate the shank, a shallow hole slightly wider than the pilot hole is needed. If the screwhead is to be set flush with or below the surface of the wood—a necessity with flathead screws but optional with other types—a still shallower hole, the diameter of the screwhead, is required. A two- or three-tier screw hole can be made with regular bits used one after the other,

but the special bit called a combination countersink *(page 63, bottom)* does the entire job in a single step.

A properly drilled hole makes driving a screw easy, if you use a screwdriver of the appropriate type and tip—and if the tip is sharp. The tip must fit snugly into the screwhead slot. Phillips screwdrivers come in three common tip sizes, flat-tip screwdrivers in four tip sizes. Using the wrong size tip may ruin the slot or damage the tip.

As important as the right size is sharpness. Rounded edges or ends will cause the screwdriver tip to slip. When wear rounds away the original sharp, straight forms of the tip, restore the original shape with a grinding wheel. Reserve your good, sharp screwdrivers for driving screws, and keep an old one for such odd jobs as opening paint cans and freeing frozen window sashes.

There are many styles and types of screwdrivers to serve special needs. Some have offset right-angle handles, extra-short or extra-long shanks, easy-to-grip knob handles, or ratchet drives. A screwdriver bit in a brace is useful for driving large screws in tight places.

For speed, a spiral-ratchet screwdriver (sometimes called by the trade name "Yankee") is a useful hand tool unless you are working in a cramped space—from screwhead to elbow, you will need more than 2½ feet for the standard model. An electric drill that you have fitted with a screwdriver bit is even faster, but it should be used only where marring the surface of the wood is of no consequence—the bit can chew into the wood if it slips from the screwhead.

Using a spiral-ratchet screwdriver. With the ratchet shifter forward, hold the chuck sleeve between thumb, index and middle fingers as you insert the bit tip into the screwhead; push the handle forward *(below, top)*. When the handle meets the sleeve, pull the handle out and push it forward in repeated strokes.

When the resistance of the wood makes it difficult to drive the screw this way, disengage the screwdriver, push the handle to the chuck sleeve and turn the locking ring counterclockwise. The screwdriver can now be used like a conventional screwdriver except that its ratchet mechanism can be left in action to ease the job: you can turn your hand and wrist counterclockwise without loosening your grip or removing the bit from the screw.

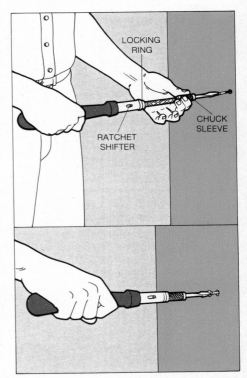

Using an electric drill. With one hand gripping the drill handle, set the palm of the other on top of the motor housing for working vertically, underneath the motor housing for working horizontally, and drive the screw at low speed. Stop the drill as soon as the screw is in place—additional revolutions will strip the threads carved in the wood or break off the screwhead.

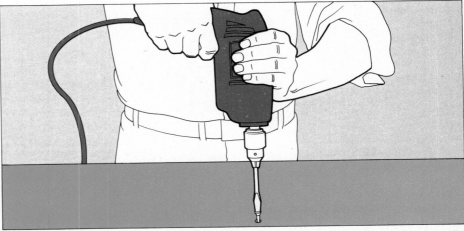

Trim Joints: Tests of Expert Craftsmanship

Trim carpentry—the craft of making neat, tightly jointed frames around doors, windows and walls—is one of the most demanding tests of woodworking skill. It requires not only mastery of the basic techniques of cutting and shaping wood, but also a repertoire of tricks for fitting and fastening the pieces. Even the most talented professional may fail to achieve a seamless fit at the first try, but must sand, plane, or saw edges—and then putty the gaps for a perfect joint.

The simplest, most common joint is the miter, which takes molding around a corner. On door and window casing, the face of the molding is cut at an angle for the miter. On inside corner joints—between the stops of a doorway, perhaps, or between baseboards that meet at the corner of a room—the ends of boards can be beveled for a miter, but a better solution may be a coped joint, in which the end of one piece (generally the shorter one) is cut to follow the molded curve of the longer one. Most miters, whether face cuts or bevels, angle at 45°. Howev-

er, other angles may be required—to case an octagonal window, for example, or to fit baseboard in a window bay.

For some moldings that meet or end in unusual places, you must work out special solutions to maintain an attractive symmetry. Stairway trim has to be joined at angles measured to match the slope of the stairs, window mullions must be mated into the shapes of casing, chair-rail ends may need to turn in toward a wall, and you may have to conceal the junction of incompatible moldings.

In all of these joints, precise marking is crucial. With casing and interior corners, always nail one piece before you mark the next, so that you will have a bench mark to measure from. Wherever possible, hold short uncut pieces in place to mark length—a faster and more accurate method than using a tape measure; on a miter cut, mark the longest point of the miter where the top edge of the molding meets the back so that you can sight the mark against the miter-box saw.

Cut moldings a fraction of an inch

longer than the measurement—1/16 inch for a short piece of casing, as much as ¼ inch for a long baseboard—because there is no good remedy for a piece that is too short. A bit of extra length, on the other hand, generally is absorbed when the piece is nailed and holds the joint tight; if your extra allowance proves too generous, some can be shaved off.

Because pieces of molding are relatively thin, they warp easily and often must be straightened as they are nailed. Most warps can be pulled straight by hand and held by nails; bad ones generally can be pulled straight by toenailing.

Trim presents additional problems. Nails tend to split it; coat them with paraffin, blunt the points with a hammer or, if needed, drill pilot holes. Furthermore, such costly wood is seldom painted but is usually given a clear finish to show its grain. This makes it difficult to hide attempts to conceal gaps and nailheads with putty. Precisely fitted joints are essential, and nails should be set where tinted putty matches the grain color.

Door and Window Casings

1 Nailing the top casing. Cut the ends of the top casing at 45° angles *(page 30)* and hold the casing in place over the head jamb—set back ⅛ inch from the inner edge of the jamb on a door, flush with the edge on most windows. Drive a nail partway through the casing into the jamb at each corner, then nail the upper edge of the casing to the header over the jamb at 12-inch intervals. Nail the lower edge of the casing to the jamb, placing the nails opposite those in the upper edge, and drive them home at each end.

2 **Fitting the side casing.** Mark the thin edge of the side-casing stock $1/16$ inch longer than is necessary for an exact fit—it extends from the bottom of the top casing miter to the stool of a window or, for a door, to the floor. Square off one end of the stock and miter the other end outward, so the thick edge is longer than the thin.

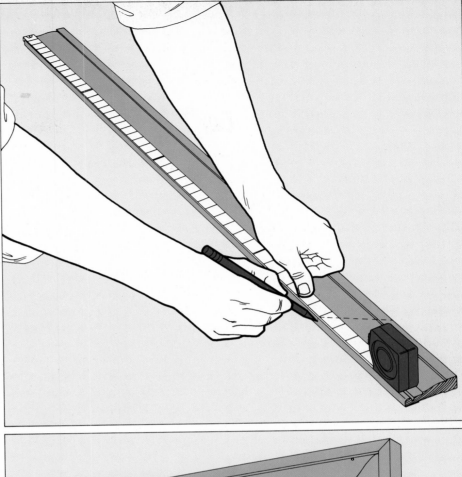

3 **Nailing up the side casing.** Fit the side casing as tightly as possible against the top casing and, at 12-inch intervals, drive nails halfway through the side casing into the studs and the jamb. Leave about ¼ inch of each of these nails protruding from the casing.

4 **Adjusting the casing.** If you find gaps, first try to close them by tapping against the sides with a hammer and wood block. If the joint remains ragged, with edges meeting at only a few points, cut along the joint line with a small backsaw called a dovetail saw, then tap the casing again.

5 **Lock-nailing the joint.** To keep the joint firmly fastened and prevent its opening when the wood shrinks, hold the side casing firmly in place and drive a fourpenny finishing nail straight down through the top casing into the side casing.

Then hold the top casing and drive a second nail horizontally through the side casing into the top casing. Use a nail set to sink these nails and then drive and sink the nails in the face of the side casing. Cover all the nailheads with putty.

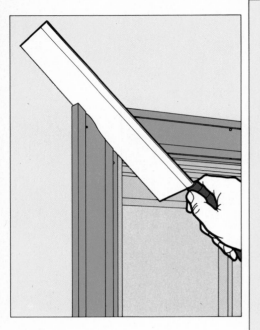

Coping a Joint

1 **Marking for a coped joint.** Butt a piece of molding into the corner and nail it to the wall. Miter the end of a second piece, angling the cut inward from the back of the piece to the front so that the cut creates a profile of the molding along the line of the cut; then mark along the curved profile line with the side of a pencil so as to make the profile more visible.

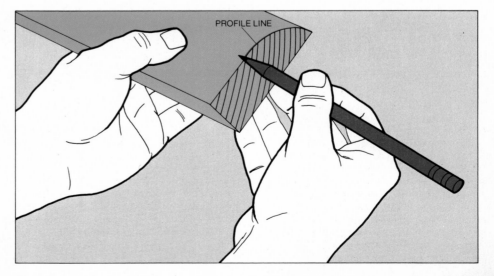

PROFILE LINE

2 Making the cut. With a coping saw aligned at a right angle to the face of the molding, cut along the profile line. The coped molding (*inset*) should now fit against the face of the molding you have installed at the corner.

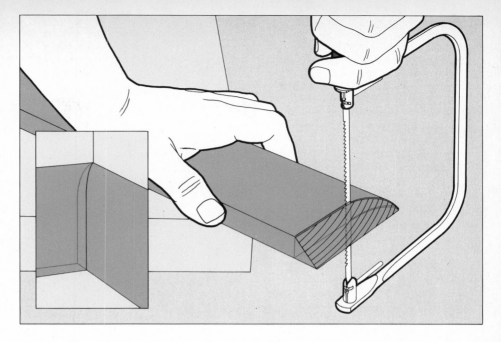

Fitting a Corner—and Fixing a Bad Fit

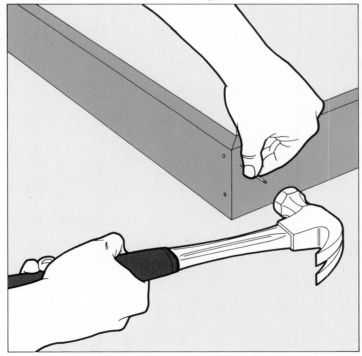

Fastening the wall molding. Miter two pieces of molding at 45° and hold them in place against the outside corner. If the joint is tight—this will occur only in the rare instance of walls meeting in a true right angle—nail the molding to studs along the wall and lock-nail the miters by driving two fourpenny finishing nails horizontally from each side. If the joint gaps, as is more likely, apply one of the remedies described at the right and on page 124 to improve the fit.

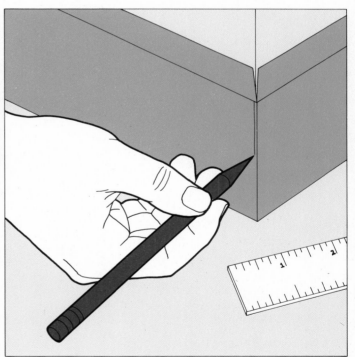

Closing a gap at the back of the joint. If the wall angle is greater than 90° and forces the joint open at the back, hold the moldings in place and measure the gap between the backs of the two pieces. If the gap is less than ¼ inch, mark a line on one piece of molding at the measured distance from the corner; if the gap is more than ¼ inch, mark half the measurement on each piece of molding. Use a block plane to shave the wood to the line or lines (*page 86*).

A gap at the front. If the wall angle is less than 90° and forces the joint open at the front, use a utility knife to shave wood—no more than ⅛ inch at a time—from the inner edge of moldings up to 4 inches wide; for larger moldings, use a coping saw but make the cuts in the same way. Start just below the top of the molding—do not shave the top, which will squeeze to a tight fit—and work down to the bottom of the joint. To correct a large gap, shave wood from both sides of the joint.

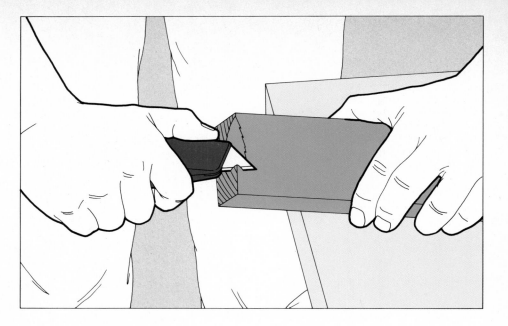

Trimming the Angles of a Staircase

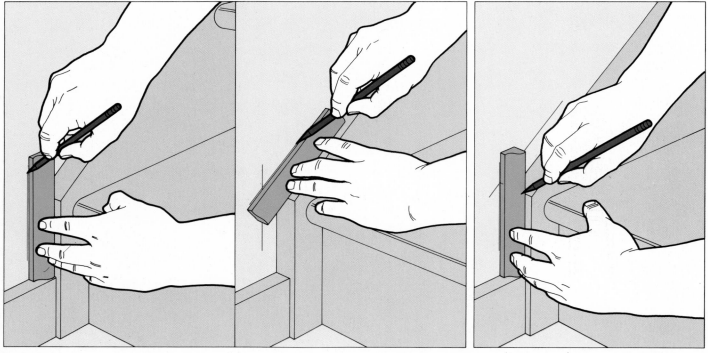

1 Marking the wall. Place the bottom of a piece of molding along one side of the angle and use the top as a straightedge to draw a line on the wall (*above, left*). Move the molding to the other side of the angle and use it to draw a second line on the wall, intersecting the first (*above, right*).

2 Marking the molding. Hold a piece of molding in position at the first side of the angle; mark the top edge of the molding at the intersection of the drawn lines on the wall, and the bottom edge at the point of the angle. Repeat the procedure with a second piece of molding held at the other side of the angle.

Set a miter box to cut each piece along a line between the marks you have made; the miter cuts will fit the moldings to the angle.

Splices and End Pieces

A miter-lap joint. Try to avoid splicing two pieces of identical molding along a single wall, but if you must make a joint on a very long wall, do so at a stud, mitering the ends of two pieces at 45° in the same direction. That is, set the miter-box saw in the same position for both the left and right pieces. Lap the cuts at a wall stud and drive two fourpenny nails through the splice into the stud.

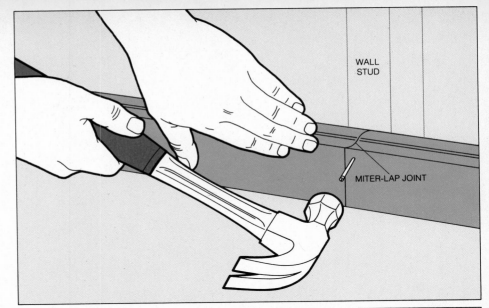

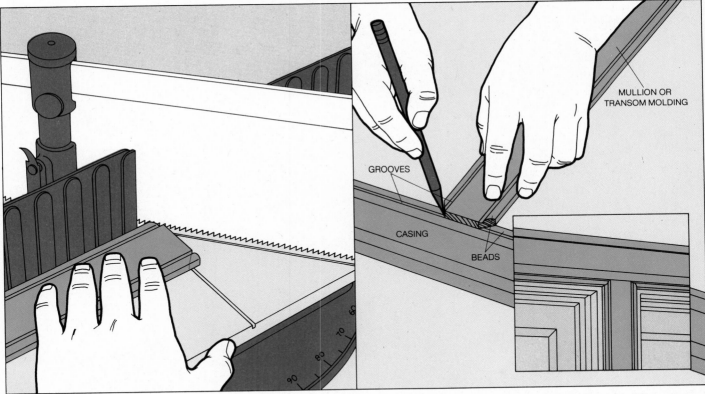

Splicing at right angles. To trim a transom over a door or a window unit containing two or more sections, you must fit special molding called mullion or transom molding at right angles into the casing. For most beaded casing, use mullion molding like that illustrated—a flat center section and edge beads the same thickness as the casing beads. Miter only the beads on each side, as indicated by the cutting line above, left. Place the mitered end of the molding over the bead of the casing and draw lines on the

casing along each miter cut (*above, right*). Using a coping saw, cut out the section of casing between the lines so that the end of the molding will fit tightly into the body of the casing, with the beads of the molding and casing forming neat miter joints (*inset*). Miter the other end similarly for a transom; for a mullion, cut the bottom end square to butt the stool.

If you cannot match beaded moldings for the technique described above, use mullion molding

thinner than the edge thickness of the casing. Do not miter it or cut into the casing; cut the mullion square to butt under the casing edge. If you use unbeaded casing and mullions—such as the smoothly curved "clamshell" style—cut a matching mullion end to a 45° point, like a fence picket, and trace and cut a mating notch into the casing. If you are unable to locate any suitable mullion molding, use a plain thin board and use a rasp to round over the end so that it curves in under the casing edge.

A mitered return. To end a run of molding that does not join another—sometimes necessary for chair rails and ceiling moldings—mark the end point on the face and miter the piece in toward the back. Miter the end of a second piece in the opposite direction, from the back in toward the face, and cut it at a 90° angle at the point where the miter cut meets the back, creating a 45°-45°-90° triangular wedge *(inset)*. Glue the wedge to the mitered end of the first piece of molding, then drill pilot holes to fit No. 19 brads and nail the wedge in place.

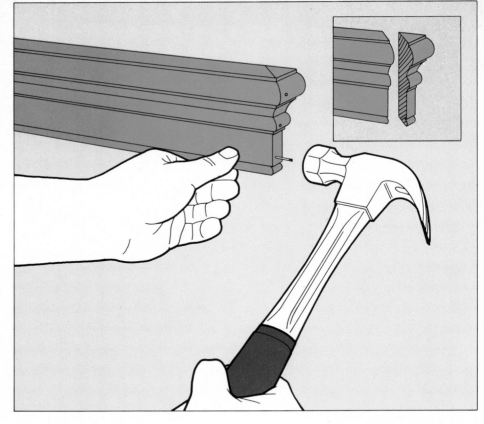

A Plinth for an Awkward Corner

A plinth block. Where different moldings meet at floor level—in this typical example, a traditional door molding and a more severely styled baseboard—cut a rectangular "plinth" block of scrap wood. Make it slightly wider, higher and thicker than the moldings and fit it to the moldings with butt joints. When you add a base shoe, miter its end to meet the outer edge of the block. A plinth block that is more than 3 inches wide can be nailed in place like a short piece of baseboard; smaller ones should be glued to the wall and to the ends of the moldings.

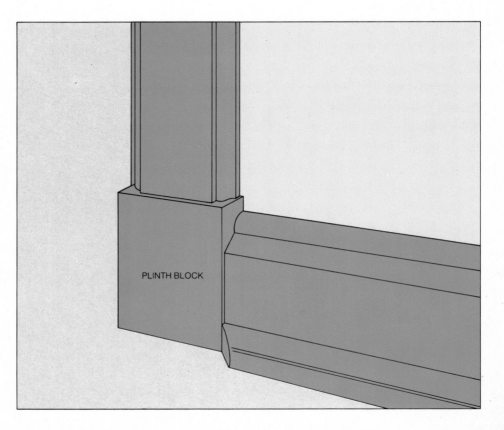

PLINTH BLOCK

A Tricky Miter Cut for a Cornice Molding

An interior corner. To make a miter joint *(inset)*, measure from corner to corner, mark the distance on the bottom edge of a length of ceiling molding and place the molding upside down in a miter box, with the bottom of the molding tight against the fence. Place the piece you want to cut on the opposite side of the saw blade from its position on the ceiling—to the right side of the blade for the left-hand corner piece, and vice versa. Set the saw for a 45° cut to the right to cut the left-hand piece, as illustrated in this example; set the handle to the left for a right-hand piece. For a neater but somewhat more difficult alternative, cope a corner piece as you would a baseboard *(pages 122-123)*.

An exterior joint. For an exterior corner *(inset)*, which cannot be coped and must be mitered, place the ceiling molding upside down and reversed in the miter box as you would for an interior joint, but do not reverse the saw's direction. Thus, cut the piece for the left side of the corner with the saw handle at the left, and the piece for the right side with the handle at the right.

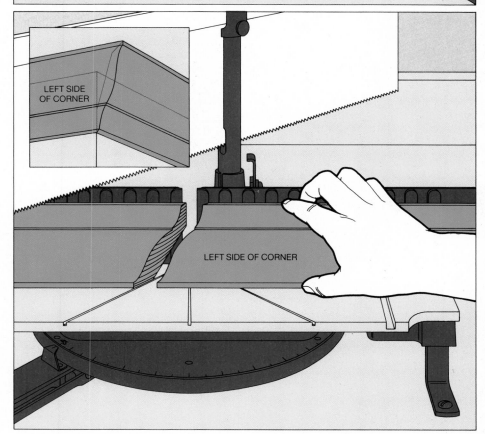

LEFT SIDE OF CORNER

BOTTOM OF MOLDING

FENCE

TOP OF MOLDING

LEFT SIDE OF CORNER

TABLE

LEFT SIDE OF CORNER

LEFT SIDE OF CORNER

Intricacies of the Old-time Woodworker's Joints

Although houses no longer are held together by strong, interlocking wooden joints, traditional woodworking joints still are needed for many special parts of a modern home. In joining those parts, simple nailing does not suffice; much stronger connections can be formed of mortises and tenons, dadoes or rabbets. These joints are used in floors, stairways and doorframes and window frames, where strength is critical; in roof soffits and exterior siding, where a weathertight seal is needed; and in interior paneling, where appearance is important.

The way two boards meet determines the type of joint preferred. Where boards meet at right angles—either end to end, as with the side and head jambs of a door, or edge to edge, as with a stairway tread and riser—either of two joints is used. The stronger is the dado joint, in which the square end of one board fits into the dado groove near the end of the other. In the slightly weaker rabbet joint, the square end fits into a matching rabbet step at the end of the other board.

Where the boards meet edge to edge, the dado and rabbet can be combined, in a joint commonly found in stairway construction. The dadoes or rabbets for these joints ordinarily must be cut on the job with a router or radial arm saw, using the techniques shown in Chapter 3, but if a number of identical joints are used, the boards can be cut by a mill.

For boards that meet edge to edge on a flat surface—hardwood floorboards, plywood subflooring, interior wall paneling, exterior siding and roof decks—the joints must combine a neat appearance with flexibility, so that the wood can contract and expand slightly as moisture and temperature change. On interior paneling and exterior siding, a variation on the rabbet joint often is used: boards are milled with a rabbet along the face of one edge and a matching rabbet along the back of the other, so that the two overlap when the paneling is installed.

Paneling, siding and flooring also can be fitted together with tongue-and-groove joints: each board has a groove milled along the center of one edge and a matching tongue (made by cutting rabbets on each side) on the other. The tongue is generally a fraction of an inch

shallower than the groove, to ensure that the board faces fit tightly together.

Because flat joints on walls and floors involve a series of boards, they require careful planning and alignment. When the boards are applied vertically on a wall, rows of 2-by-4 blocks must be nailed horizontally between the studs, one quarter, one half and three quarters of the way up the wall. To make sure a thin, unsightly board is not left at the end of the job, the width of the boards being used (plus any gap) should be divided into the length of the wall or floor. If the amount left over is less than 2 inches, both the first and last boards should be trimmed equally so that both are more than 2 inches wide. Where the joint between a board and a wall will be

exposed, the board may need to be scribed and sawed or planed to the irregular contour of the wall; and in hardwood paneling, pilot holes must be drilled to keep the entering nails from splitting the wood.

The third type of joint, the mortise and tenon (pages 132-133), is used when two boards meet, face up, at right angles, as in a window sash or paneled door. The projecting tenon at the end of one board fits into the mortise hole in the other board and is secured by glue or dowels. Mortise-and-tenon joints are less common in new window sashes and doors because modern glues and machine woodworking have supplanted them to some extent, but they may be needed in making repairs on old woodwork.

Three Basic Right-Angle Joints

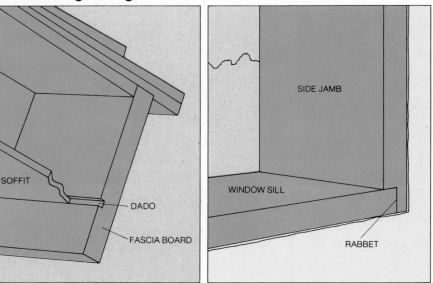

A dado joint. Under the eave of this house roof, the edge of the plywood soffit fits into a groove, or dado, in the back of the fascia board, forming a strong, weathertight joint. The dado—its depth ordinarily one third to one half the thickness of the fascia board—prevents the soffit from moving up or down; the joint could work loose only if the soffit and fascia board pulled apart. Dado joints also fit the top edge of stair risers to the undersides of treads. The same joint can be used between the ends of boards: the top and bottom jambs of a window and the top jamb of a doorframe often fit into dadoes in the side jambs.

A rabbet joint. At the bottom of this window frame, the sill fits into a step, or rabbet, in the side jamb. Rabbet joints like this one also are used at the tops of doorframes and window frames, where the ends of the top jamb meet the side jambs. The same joint can be used between the edges of boards: the back edge of a stairway tread may fit into a rabbet at the bottom of the riser above it, for example.

Rabbet joints are somewhat weaker than dado joints, because nails alone are not as strong as the combination of a dado groove and nails; however, because a rabbet joint forms a square corner, it can fit into a stair carriage or a doorframe, and a dado joint cannot.

A rabbet-and-dado joint. On this staircase, the back of each tread is rabbeted to fit into a dado near the bottom of each riser. The resulting rabbet-and-dado joint combines the best of both types: it is nearly as strong as a dado, but can be made at the edge of a board like a rabbet. In such a stairway, the tops of the risers and the fronts of the treads often are joined in the same way, but as a matter of convenience only; a dado would work just as well there.

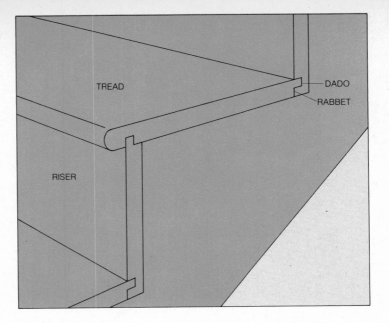

Flexible Joints for Walls and Floors

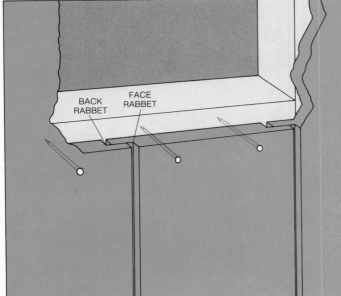

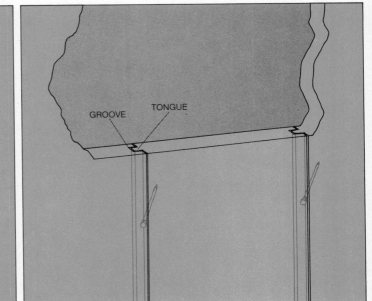

Rabbet joints. In this interior-wall paneling, each board has a rabbet along one edge of the exposed face and another along the opposite edge at the back. The projection at the face overlaps the back rabbet to conceal cracks; there is a gap—called a reveal—between each projection and the body of the next board, to allow boards to expand and contract without buckling or splitting. The same joint can be used for horizontal paneling or, without the gaps between boards, for weathertight exterior siding.

Tongue-and-groove joints. In this paneling, each board has a groove milled along the center of one edge and a matching tongue along the other. The tongues and grooves interlock in nearly invisible joints and the boards are fastened with "blind nails," which are driven at an angle through the tongue of each board so that they are hidden by the groove of the next board. Tongue-and-groove joints are stronger and more flexible than rabbet joints. They are used for wood flooring, because they resist squeaking and warping; for plywood subflooring, because they eliminate the need for rows of blocking to support the edges of the sheets; and for exterior siding, because they resist air infiltration.

Assembling a Right-Angle Joint

A dado joint. Slip the end of one board into a dado on a second board (in this example the first board is the top jamb of a doorframe, the second is a side jamb), then drive pairs of nails in V patterns through the dado, from the second board into the first (*inset*). The opposing angles of the nails help keep the joint tight.

If the first board is more than ½ inch thick and so warped that it will not slip easily into the dado, plane the end of the board down; forcing such a board into place can cause it to split.

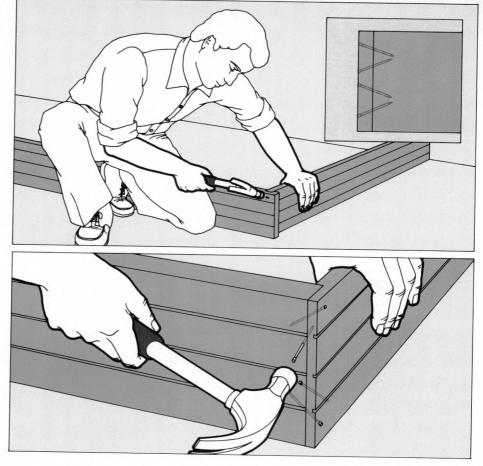

A rabbet joint. For a joint commonly used to fasten doorjambs and window jambs together, fit and nail the end of one board into a rabbet in a second board. Near the edges of the rabbeted board, drive a pair of nails in a V pattern through the rabbet into the end of the unrabbeted board, angling the nails toward the middle of the board; brace the other end against a wall to keep the joint tight while you nail. Then drive a second pair of nails through the unrabbeted board into the end of the rabbeted one (*right*), starting the nails near the middle of the board and angling them out toward the edges.

Installing a Set of Rabbeted Panels

1 Aligning the first boards. To prepare the wall, nail a plumb starter board to 2-by-4 blocks, fastened between the studs in three horizontal rows, and also to the top plate and sole plate. If you are also paneling the adjacent wall, rabbet both edges of the starter—a normal 1-inch rabbet on the left edge, and on the right edge a rabbet equal to the thickness of a board and the width of the planned gap between boards. If you are paneling only one side of a room, do not rabbet the right edge; instead, fit the edge to the adjacent wall.

Set a ¼-inch plywood spacer into the left-hand rabbet of the starter board near the top of the wall, slide the edge of the next board against the spacer and drive two finishing nails through the face of the new board—not through the rabbets—into the top plate. Place the spacer into the rabbet near the bottom of the board and nail the board to the bottom plate; then nail the board to each of the blocks. Repeat this procedure for each of the succeeding four boards.

SPACER

2 × 4 BLOCKS

2 **Keeping the boards vertical.** Every six boards, fasten the top of a board with only one nail, then hold a level in the rabbet near the bottom of the board. Swing the board from side to side until it is plumb, then nail the board to the sole plate, the top plate and the horizontal blocks in the normal way.

At the left end of the wall, install the starter board of the adjacent wall (*Step 1*) if you plan to put paneling on the other side of the corner. Scribe and cut the last board so that it will fit snugly into the rabbet of the starter board (or against the wall, if you are not paneling the adjacent wall), then nail it in place.

Fitting and Nailing Tongue-and-Groove Joints

1 **Driving the boards together.** On a wall, align the first board against an adjacent wall, with the tongue facing out; plumb it with a level and nail through its face into the top and sole plates and into horizontal blocks like those used for rabbeted paneling (*opposite, bottom*). On a floor or roof, align the board by measuring from a reference point, such as the bottom of a wall. Slide the groove of the next board onto the tongue of the first one and fit the groove of a hammering block—a short scrap of tongue-and-groove board—over the tongue of the new board near one end. Strike the block firmly with a mallet, driving the new board onto the tongue of the previous one; slide the block along the board as you work so that the board seats evenly.

2 **Nailing the tongue.** Drive nails at a 45° angle partway through the base of the tongue, where it meets the body of the board, into the blocks or structural members behind the board; sink the nails with a nail set, taking care not to to splinter the tongue. If a board is more than 8 inches wide, face-nail it through the middle; narrower tongue-and-groove boards need not be face-nailed.

On a vertical surface, plumb every sixth board as you would a rabbeted one (*Step 2, above*) and adjust it by driving one end tight with the hammering block; on a horizontal surface, measure from the edge of the board to the reference point. At the end of the wall or floor, cut off the tongue edge of the next-to-last board and install it by nailing through its face. Scribe the last board on the tongue edge to match it to the wall (*page 47, bottom*), cut it along the scribed line and face-nail it, with the groove against the cut edge of the next-to-last board.

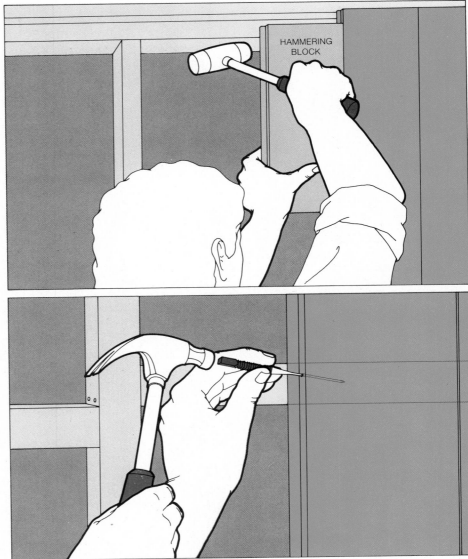

HAMMERING BLOCK

Setting a Tenon into a Mortise

In a mortise-and-tenon joint, the projecting tenon of one piece fits so snugly into the rectangular mortise hole of the other that the two pieces are joined together almost as strongly as if they were a single piece of wood. Such strength is particularly important in window sashes and paneled doors, which are subjected to repeated stresses that would quickly pull apart a simple butt joint. Factory-made mortise-and-tenon joints like the one on page 108 rarely need to be replaced or even repaired.

The tenon is always made on the shorter of the two pieces—generally the horizontal rail of a door or window. This is done so that the short piece can be clamped vertically in a vise when it is sawed and chiseled (pages 94-95), as a long piece could not be.

To make a strong, precise joint, you will need a special tool called a mortising gauge, which has two sharp points that can be set to mark both sides of a mortise at once and to transfer the marks to the tenon without changing the adjustment.

Modern mortise-and-tenon joints generally are fastened by glue alone, but the old-fashioned technique of using a crosswise dowel to pin such a joint together still has its uses. To mend a joint that has popped loose, you sometimes can drive the pieces back together, drill a hole (page 65) through the joint and glue in a dowel; the alternative—disassembling the joint, then cleaning and regluing it—is difficult and time-consuming.

A blind mortise-and-tenon joint. At the corner of this window sash, the mortise in the vertical stile at left has a width equal to one third the thickness of the stile and a depth equal to three quarters the stile width, a design that gives maximum strength. At the end of the horizontal stile at right, the rectangular, projecting tenon is ⅛ inch shorter than the depth of the mortise to allow space for glue.

The sides of the tenon, called cheeks, fit snugly between the wide inner faces of the mortise, to take advantage of the strength of a joint glued between the long grain of rail and stile. The shoulders of the mortise and of the tenon, on the bodies of the boards, fit together flush on all sides; they brace the stile against the rail and allow the end of the rail to hide the mortise.

The same joint is used between the rails and stiles at the edges of paneled doors, as well as between the intermediate rails and the outer stiles; it also is used between muntins, which divide the panes of a window.

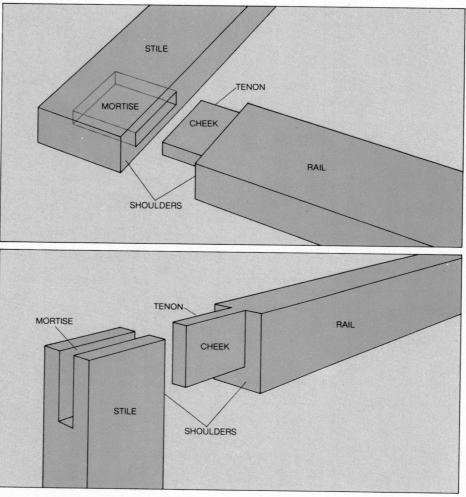

An open mortise-and-tenon joint. Often used at the corners of window sashes, this joint is a simpler alternative to the blind joint. An open mortise—a U-shaped cavity cut at the end of the stile with a mortise chisel or drill-press attachment—receives the tenon of the rail. Shoulders on the sides of the tenon strengthen the joint, as they do in a blind mortise-and-tenon joint, but the end of the tenon and one side of it are flush with the end and the outside edge of the stile. The joint shown here is secured with glue alone, but dowels or metal pins running through both mortise and tenon sometimes are used instead of glue or in addition to it.

Assembling the Joint

1 **Setting the mortising gauge.** Choose a mortise chisel whose width is one third to one half the thickness of the wood to be joined; rest the chisel on a workbench, the tip overhanging the edge of the bench. Loosen the thumbscrew atop the gauge fence, hold the gauge to the chisel tip and set the gauge points to the chisel-tip width by turning the adjusting thumbscrew at the end of the bar. (If you are using a drill-press mortising attachment (*page 74*), set the gauge to the width of the chisel of the attachment.)

Hold the gauge against the edge of one board, slide the bar through the fence until the points are centered on the board and tighten the fence thumbscrew. Use the gauge to mark mortise (*page 73*) and tenon (*page 94*); chisel out the mortise and saw the tenon in the ordinary way.

2 **Test-fitting the joint.** Clamp the mortised board horizontally in a woodworking vise and push the tenon into the mortise, tapping it gently with a mallet if necessary. If you meet strong resistance, pull the tenon out and look for shiny spots on its cheeks, signs of bulges in the mortise or tenon. Use a chisel to pare away the shiny spots, working across the grain with the bevel facing up (*page 72*), then test the joint again. Pare the tenon until you can force it into the mortise, then separate the pieces.

If the tenon is loose in the mortise, glue and clamp a thin layer of wood to one or both cheeks, let the glue set and pare the tenon.

3 **Assembling the joint.** Spread glue on the tenon with your finger and inside the mortise with a thin scrap of wood; to prevent excess glue from being squeezed out when the joint is assembled, use only enough glue to barely cloud the surface of the wood and do not glue the base of the tenon near the shoulders. Slide the tenon into the mortise (if you are assembling a window sash or a door with several joints, glue and assemble all of them at once) and set the pieces flat on a workbench.

Hold the boards together with a long bar clamp, using scrap blocks of wood to protect the surface; pinch the mortise around the cheeks of the tenon with a C clamp. Check the joint with a framing square, then tighten the clamps.

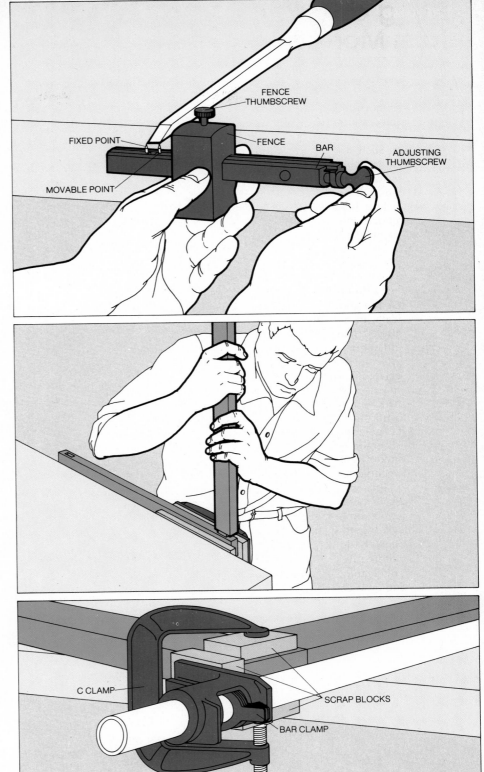

FENCE THUMBSCREW

FIXED POINT

FENCE

BAR

ADJUSTING THUMBSCREW

MOVABLE POINT

C CLAMP

SCRAP BLOCKS

BAR CLAMP

Picture Credits

Credits for the pictures from left to right are separated by semicolons, from top to bottom by dashes. The drawings were created by Jack Arthur, Roger C. Essley, Fred Holz, Dick Lee, Joan S. McGurren and Bill McWilliams.

Cover: Fil Hunter. 6: Stephen R. Brown. 9,10: Frederic F. Bigio from B-C Graphics. 14-21: Frederic F. Bigio from B-C Graphics. 22-27: Ray Skibinski. 28-31: Eduino Pereira. 33: Robert Perron, Ric Weinschenk, architect. 34: A. F. Kersting, London—John T. Hill. 35: Robert Perron, Thomas V. S. Cullins, architect—Robert Perron, Steven Conger, architect. 36: John Bethell, St. Albans, John Chute, architect—Taylor Lewis and Associates, woodwork by William Buckland. 37: Armen Kachaturian, Stephen Levine, architect. 38: Marvin Rand, Charles and Henry Greene, architects—John T. Hill, Edward Larrabee Barnes, architect; John T. Hill, Eliot Noyes and Associates, architects. 39: Aldo Ballo, Milan, Marcello D'Olivo, architect. 40: Colonial Williamsburg Foundation, woodwork by Richard Bayliss; Aldo Ballo, Milan, staircase designed by Giancarlo Nocentini. 42-45: Frederic F. Bigio from B-C Graphics. 46-51: Walter Hilmers Jr. 52,53: John Massey. 54-59: Frederic F. Bigio from B-C Graphics. 60: Stephen R. Brown. 62-69: Walter Hilmers Jr. 70-74: Whitman Studio, Inc. 75: Illustration from *Colonial Craftsmen*, © 1965 Edwin Tunis, Thomas Y. Crowell. 76-79: Forte, Inc. 80: Stephen R. Brown. 82-87: Peter McGinn. 88-91: Walter Hilmers Jr. 92-95: John Massey. 96-99: Gerry Gallagher. 100,101: James Robert Long. 102-107: John Massey. 108: Stephen R. Brown. 110,111: Frederic F. Bigio from B-C Graphics. 114-119: Frederic F. Bigio from B-C Graphics. 120-127: John Massey. 128-133: Walter Hilmers Jr.

Acknowledgments

The index/glossary for this book was prepared by Louise Hedberg. The editors also wish to thank the following: Harold Ashton, Donohoe Construction, Alexandria, Va.; Tommy Bargeron, Moultrie, Ga.; Ed Bishop, Manassas, Va.; Wanda Cast, U.S. Forest Service, Arlington, Va.; J. W. Chabot, Alexandria, Va.; Peter Danko, Pond Gallery, Alexandria, Va.; Zachary Domike, Cohen, Haft, Holtz, Kerxton, Karabekien Associates, Silver Spring, Md.; Donald T. Duffey, Stanley Power Tools, Newburn, N.C.; Peter C. Eggers, Woden Woods, Denver, Co.; Riley W. Eldridge, Rockwell International, Hyattsville, Md.; Ivan J. Hahn and Carlton F. Moe, DeWalt Division of Black and Decker, Lancaster, Pa.; Harry Harwood, Alexandria, Va.; Stella Hawkins, Preservation Resource Group, Inc., Springfield, Va.; Blake Hays, Georgia Agrirama Development Authority, Tifton, Ga.; Carol Helderlein, Rockwell International, Pittsburgh, Pa.; Bruce Hoadley, Amherst, Mass.; Joseph M. Honeychunk, Joint Carpentry Apprenticeship Committee, Upper Marlboro, Md.; Peter Kramer, Washington, Va.; Ian Kirby, Hoosuck Design and Woodworking School, North Adams, Mass.; Bill McCredie, National Forest Products Association, Washington, D.C.; Nathaniel Neblett, National Trust for Historic Preservation, Washington, D.C.; Fred Saks, Smoot Lumber Company, Alexandria, Va.; Karl Seemuller, Riverton, N.J.; Leland Schwartz, States News Service, Washington, D.C.; Sansbury Jay Sweeney, Memphis, Tenn.; Gary Thomas, T. A. Edison High School, Alexandria, Va.; Frank Trinca, C. M. Peletz Company, Burlingame, Calif.; James Vipond, Washington, D.C.; Gordie Whittington, Vicksburg, Miss.; Wayne Wilt, Herndon, Va.

The following persons also gave assistance in the preparation of this book: Stephen Brown, Peggy Eastman, Wendy Murphy and Robert Phillips.

Index/Glossary